RIO DE JANEIRO
Everyman MapGuides

KU-626-971

Welcome to Rio de Janeiro!

This opening fold-out contains a general map of Rio de Janeiro to help you visualise the 6 large districts discussed in this guide, and 4 pages of valuable information, handy tips and useful addresses.

Discover Rio de Janeiro through 6 districts and 6 maps

A Centro
B Lapa / Santa Teresa / Glória
C Catete / Flamengo / Laranjeiras / Cosme Velho
D Botafogo / Urca / Copacabana
E Ipanema / Leblon / Lagoa / Jardim Botânico
F Barra de Tijuca / Zona Oeste

For each district there is a double-page of addresses (restaurants – listed in ascending order of price – cafés, bars, music venues and shops), followed by a fold-out map for the relevant area with the essential places to see (indicated on the map by a star ★). These places are by no means all that Rio has to offer, but to us they are unmissable. The grid-referencing system (**A** B2) makes it easy for you to pinpoint addresses quickly on the map.

Transportation and hotels in Rio de Janeiro
The last fold-out consists of a transportation map and 4 pages of practical information that include a selection of hotels.

Index
Lists all the street names, sites and monuments featured in this guide.

MUSIC

Bossa nova: samba with jazz inflections.
Choro/chorinho: virtuoso instrumental style played on the *cavaquinho* (small guitar), flute and *pandeiro* (tambourine).
Forró: northeastern rhythm danced in couples.
MPB (*Musica Popular Brasileira*): generic name for modern pop music.
Pagode: derivative of samba, with humorous lyrics and light percussion.
Samba de roda / Samba de mesa: small group playing samba informally around a table.

SUGARLOAF MOUNTAIN

February
Carnival
→ *Carnival Sat – Ash Wednesday (public holidays)*
March
Holy Week
→ *Good Friday*
Reenactment of Christ's Passion under the Arches of Lapa (**B** D2).
April
Dia de Tiradentes
→ *April 21 (public holiday)*
Commemoration of the martyr of independence.
June
Festas juninas
→ *June 13, 24 and 29*
Folkloric festivals connected to saints John, Anthony and Peter: dances in wedding clothes and peasant dress, bonfires, fireworks.
July
Arte de Portas Abertas
→ *July, Aug or Sep (Fri-Sun)*
Artists' studios in Santa Teresa open their doors to the public.

Anima mundi
→ *July*
International festival of animated movies.
September
Festival do Rio
→ *2 weeks in Aug-Sep*
The most important festival of Latin-American cinema.
Dia da Independência
→ *Sep 7 (national holiday)*
Brazilian Independence Day.
October
Dia de N. S. da Aparecida
→ *Oct 12 (public holiday)*
Masses in honor of Brazil's patron saint.
November
Proclamação da República
→ *Nov 15 (public holiday)*
Commemoration of the proclamation of the Republic.
Zumbi dos Palmares
→ *Nov 20 (public holiday)*
Black awareness day, in memory of the slaves' resistance movement.

December
Ano novo
→ *Dec 31*
Spectacular fireworks on Copacabana beach, watched by 2 million people! Offerings to Lemanjá, the goddess of the sea in *candomblé* (Afro-Brazilian cult). White clothes obligatory!

OPENING HOURS

Stores and offices
Usually Mon-Fri 9am–6pm, Sat 9am–1pm.
Shopping malls
Mon-Sat 10am–10pm, Sun 3–9pm
'Lojas de conveniências'
Well-stocked grocery stores in gas stations open daily, 24 hours.
Banks
Mon-Fri 10am–4pm.
Museums
Tue-Fri 10am–6pm, Sat-Sun 2–6pm.

TIMELINE

1502: arrival of the Portuguese in Rio.
1555–1567: attempted colonization by the French.
March 1, 1565: Rio founded by Estácio de Sá
1763: Rio made capital of the colony.
1808–21: the King of Portugal exiled to Rio.
1822: proclamation of independence by Pedro I son of João VI.
1840: enthronement of Pedro II.
1888: abolition of slavery
1889: establishment of the first Republic.
1960: transfer of the capital to Brasilia.

ARCHITECTURE

Colonial baroque
Behind the simple façades, *talha* (sculpted wooden decor) holds sway, in the form of angels, foliage and gilding; **Igreja de S. Francisco da Penitência** (**A** D4).
Neoclassicism
Introduced by Grandjean de Montigny, architect of the French Mission (1816) commissioned by the King of Portugal to spruce up the city; **Casa França-Brasil** (**A** D2).
Modernism
Under the influence of Le Corbusier, a whole generation of architects and city planners (Alfonso Reidy, Lúcio Costa, Oscar Niemeyer, Roberto Burle Marx) took to working with concrete, structures built on piles, sun shields and curved lines; **Palácio Capanema** (**A** E4).

PRAIA DE IPANEMA / POSTO 9

CITY PROFILE

- 2nd largest city in Brazil
- 6 million inh. ■ 3 hrs behind GMT; 2 hrs ahead of New York ■ Summer (Dec-March): 86°F; winter (June-Aug): 64°F; spring/autumn: 77°F
- $1 = 2.50 R$ (real); £1 = 4.50 R$ (real)

THE DISTRICTS IN RIO DE JANEIRO

(Map of Rio de Janeiro showing districts: SÃO JOÃO DE MERITI, NILÓPOLIS, PAVUNA, JUIZ DE FORA, ILHA DO GOVERNADOR, INHAÚMA, BAÍA DE GUANABARA, CAMPOS, NITERÓI, CENTRO, CAMPO GRANDE, JACAREPAGUÁ, PARQUE NACIONAL DA TIJUCA, BOTAFOGO, PÃO DE AÇUCAR, LAGOA, LEBLON, COPACABANA, SÃO CONRADO, IPANEMA, RECREIO DOS BANDEIRANTES, BARRA DA TIJUCA, BARRA DE GUARATIBA, OCEANO ATLÂNTICO, SÃO PAULO, AVENIDA BRASIL, LINHA VERMELHA, LINHA AMARELA, SERRA DA CARIOCA, BR101, BR116)

TOURIST INFO

Riotur
Copacabana (D B3)
→ Av. Princesa Isabel, 183
Tel. 2541-7522
Daily 9am–6pm (summer: Sat-Sun 8am–6pm)
Centro (A D3)
→ Rua da Assembléia, 10 9th floor Tel. 2217-7575
Mon-Fri 9am–6pm
Information point (D A5)
→ Posto 6 (corner of Av. Atlântica and Rainha Elizabete) Mon-Fri noon–6pm
Alô Rio (Hotline)
→ Tel. 0800 707-1808 (in English) Mon-Fri 9am–6pm
British Consulate (C F2)
→ Praia do Flamengo, 284 Tel. 2555-9600 (out of hours emergency telephone: +55 (21) 9646 6692) www.britishembassy.gov.uk
US Consulate (A E4)
→ Av. Presidente Wilson, 147 Tel. 3823-2000 www.consulado-americano-rio.org.br

SAFETY

A few common-sense rules: carry only the strict minimum of cash, especially on the beach, and leave your passport in the hotel (carry a photocopy). Be warned that it is dangerous to walk on the beach at night.
Tourist police (E C4)
→ Av. Afrânio de Melo Franco Tel. 3399-7170

INTERNET

Rio de Janeiro online
→ www.riodejaneiro-turismo.com.br
Rio's tourist office.
→ www.turisrio.rj.gov.br
Government tourist office.
→ www.ipanema.com
Entertaining website on Rio.
Internet cafés
Around R$10/hr.
Café com Letras (E C4)
→ Av. Bartolomeu Mitre, 297 Tel. 2249-3079

Daily 8am–10pm
Letras e Expressões (E D4)
→ Rua Visconde de Pirajá, 276 Tel. 2521-6110 Mon-Sat 8am–midnight (2am Fri-Sat)
Central Fone (A D4)
→ By the Carioca subway exit Tel. 2220-3841 Mon-Fri 9am–9pm, Sat 10am–4pm

TELEPHONE

For intercity or international calls, use a private phone company: Embratel (21), Intelig (23) or Telemar (31).
Rio de Janeiro–UK/US
→ 00 + company code + country code + number (without initial 0)
Intercity calls
→ 0 + company code + state code + number
UK/US–Rio de Janeiro
→ 00 (UK) / 011 (US) + 55 (Brazil) + 21 (state of Rio) + number
Useful numbers
Emergency
→ Tel. 190

Fire service
→ Tel. 193
Directory enquiries
→ Tel. 102
Pharmacy 24/7
→ Tel. 2275-3847

BUDGET

Restaurants
Around R$20 for a meal (for two people in a down-market restaurant).
Museums
Around R$5 to enter.
Accommodation
Around R$120 for a basic double room, R$250 upward in a luxury hotel.
Currency exchange
In casas de câmbio, hotels and some cash dispensers.

DIARY OF EVENTS

January
Dia de São Sebastião
→ Jan 20 (public holiday)
Processions in honor of the city's patron's saint.

Welcome to Rio de Janeiro!

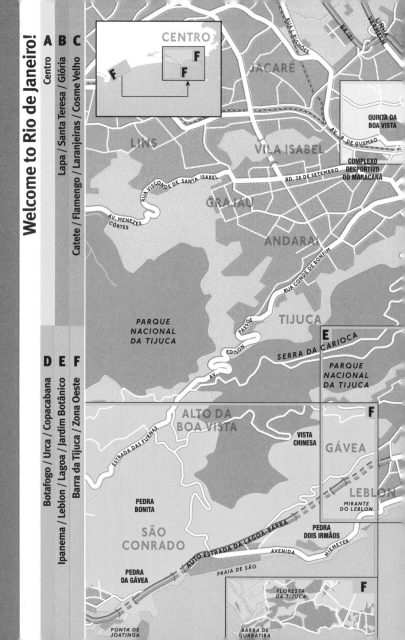

A Centro

B Lapa / Santa Teresa / Glória

C Catete / Flamengo / Laranjeiras / Cosme Velho

D Botafogo / Urca / Copacabana

E Ipanema / Leblon / Lagoa / Jardim Botânico

F Barra da Tijuca / Zona Oeste

CENTRO

F

F

F

F

RUA BULHÕES

BR. 101

LINHA VERMELHA

JACARÉ

QUINTA DA BOA VISTA

AV. B. DE GUSMÃO

COMPLEXO DESPORTIVO DO MARACANÃ

LINS

VILA ISABEL

RUA VISCONDE DE SANTA ISABEL

BD. 28 DE SETEMBRO

GRAJAÚ

AV. MENEZES CÔRTES

ANDARAÍ

RUA CONDE DE BONFIM

PARQUE NACIONAL DA TIJUCA

AV. PASSOS

TIJUCA

AV. EDISON

SERRA DA CARIOCA

E

PARQUE NACIONAL DA TIJUCA

ALTO DA BOA VISTA

F

VISTA CHINESA

GÁVEA

ESTRADA DAS FURNAS

PEDRA BONITA

LEBLON

MIRANTE DO LEBLON

SÃO CONRADO

PEDRA DOIS IRMÃOS

AUTO ESTRADA DA LAGOA-BARRA

AVENIDA NIEMEYER

PEDRA DA GÁVEA

PRAIA DE SÃO

FLORESTA DA TIJUCA

F

PONTA DE JOATINGA

BARRA DE GUARATIBA

The business district, a hive of activity by day and a ghost town by night, abounds in contrasts: tower blocks loom over the splendid baroque churches left over from colonial Rio, while the Avenida Presidente Vargas and Rio Branco thrust their way through the urban sprawl and open up views of the bay. The streets intertwine to form a maze around the bustling Saara market. To the south lies the Largo (square) da Carioca, a stage for fire-and-brimstone preachers among the diverse array of skyscrapers, while Cinelândia celebrates the splendors of the Roaring Twenties. Beyond the railroad station is the North Zone and the Maracanã, temple of Brazilian soccer.

TEN KAI

MALA E CUIA

RESTAURANTS

Bistro do Paço (A E3)
→ Praça XV de Novembro, 48
Tel. 2262-3613
Mon-Fri 11.30am–7.30pm,
Sat-Sun noon–7pm
The bustle of the Rua Primeiro de Março is completely left behind in the patio of the Paço Imperial. The bistro to one side serves quiches, copious salads and filling sandwiches, either as fast food or for a more leisurely meal. À la carte R$8–10.

Golositá (A E3)
→ Av. Erasmo Braga, 115, 4th floor (Forum) Tel. 2292-4158 Mon-Fri 11am–4pm
A delightful surprise on the fourth floor of the Law Courts (Forum). Like a hanging garden, the huge covered terrace bedecked with green plants provides a haven from the busy streets. Mouthwatering buffet of fish and meat dishes. R$2.80/100g (3½ oz).

Bar Luiz (A D4)
→ Rua da Carioca, 39
Tel. 2262-6900 Mon-Sat 11am–11pm, Sun noon–6pm
A neighborhood institution (founded in 1887) of distant German-Swiss origin that still continues the tradition of Bratwurst, sauerkraut and Kassler (pork chops). The bar's lasting success is also down to its iced draft beer. Main course R$17–25.

Ten Kai (A D4)
→ Rua Senador Dantas, 75-H
Tel. 2240-5898
Mon-Fri 11am–4pm
At the dusk of the narrow dining room, Sussumu Shimizu cuts and prepares sushi, sashimi, yaki soba (vegetable pasta), tempura and yakimeshi (Japanese fried rice). The combinados offer a selection of raw-fish tidbits. Combinado (for two) R$59.

Mala e Cuia (A E4)
→ Av. Presidente Wilson, 123
Tel. 2524-5143
Mon-Fri 11am–3.30pm
A veritable culinary embassy for Minas Gerais, the Brazilian state renowned for its hearty home cooking. A flat rate provides a selection from a dozen piping hot dishes, as well as traditional desserts (pumpkin milk jam, guava jelly with coconut etc.). To wash them down, vintage cachaças and tropical fruit liqueurs (genipapo, graviola). Buffet R$16.

Cais do Oriente (A D3)
→ Rua Visconde de Itaboraí, 8
Tel. 2203-0178
Tue-Sat noon–midnight,
Sun-Mon noon–4pm

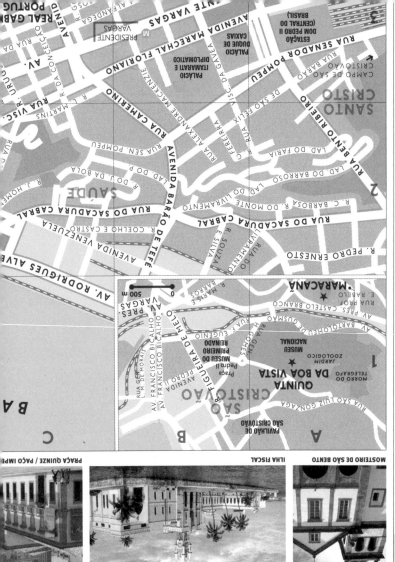

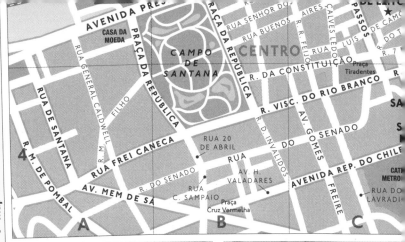

MUSEU NACIONAL DE BELAS ARTES

PALÁCIO GUSTAVO CAPANEMA

★ **Mosteiro
de São Bento** (A D2)
→ *Rua Dom Gerardo, 68
(ramp) or 40 (elevator, 5th
floor) Tel. 2291-7122
Daily 7am–noon, 2–6pm*
This monastery, built in
honor of São Bento
(1617–69), is one of Rio's
most important baroque
buildings. The austere
façade of its church hides
a fabulously ornate interior,
replete with floral gilt
compositions and cherubs.

★ **Ilha Fiscal** (A F2)
→ *Av. Alfredo Agache
Tel. 3870-6819
Espaço Cultural da Marinha:
Tue-Sun noon–5pm.
Excursion to Ilha Fiscal:
Thu-Sun 1pm, 2.30pm, 4pm*

In 1889, the blue-green
neo-Gothic palace that
seemingly floats on water
witnessed the last waltz to
be played under Imperial
rule. It can be reached from
the quay of the Espaço
Cultural da Marinha,
devoted to the history of
Brazil's naval forces.

★ **Praça Quinze** (A E3)
→ *Paço Imperial Praça XV
de Novembro, 48
Tel. 2533-4407
Tue-Sun noon–6.30pm*
This square, once the heart
of colonial Rio, owes its
name to the date of the
declaration of the Republic
(November 15, 1889). It is
the site of the Paço Imperial,
a modest palace (1743) that

was home to the Portuguese
court from 1808, and is now
a center for contemporary
art. To the north, the Arco
de Teles opens onto a maze
of alleyways, with the
sobrados (two-story
buildings) typical of old Rio.

★ **Real Gabinete
Português de Leitura**
(A C3)
→ *Rua Luís de Camões, 30
Tel. 2221-3138*
A superb library, founded
by Portuguese émigrés in
1837, with no less than
350,000 volumes! It is set
in a neo-Manuelin building
(1887) with stained-glass
windows and columns
embellished with cable
molding.

★ **Museu Nacional
de Belas Artes** (A D4)
→ *Av. Rio Branco, 199
Tel. 2240-0068
Tue-Fri 10am–6pm,
Sat-Sun 2–6pm*
The National Art Muse[um]
displays works from th[e]
French artistic mission
(1816), as well as 19th-
century paintings such [as]
First Mass by Vítor Mei[reles]
(1832–1903), and the e[pic]
Battle of Avaí by Pedro
Américo (1843–1905). [The]
major figures of the 20th
century are also
represented: the Mode[rnist]
painter Tarsila do Ama[ral]
(*Self-portrait in a Red C[oat*)]
and Candido Portinari
(*Café*, 1935). See also t[he]

CHURCH IN GLÓRIA

SANTA TERESA

CARNIVAL PROCESSION IN THE SAMBÓDROMO

THE RIO CARNIVAL

Above all, this is a contest! The 14 biggest samba schools (with 4,000 dancers each) parade in the Sambódromo (**B** A2) Sun and Mon (9pm–5am), the smaller ones on Sat and Tue. On weekends they all open their HQs for rehearsals. Meanwhile, the *blocos de rua*, neighborhood schools, parade in the streets.

→ *Salgueiro: R. Silva Teles 104, Tijuca Tel. 2288-3065* The nearest school to the city center.

→ *Mangueira: R. Visconde de Niterói 1072, Mangueira Tel. 2567-4637* The most popular school.

MEDIA

Press

...e two dailies with the biggest circulation, *Jornal ... Brasil* and *O Globo*, ...blish a cultural ...pplement on Fridays.

Magazines

...ja, the most widely read ...eekly, comes out on ...ndays, with a leisure ...pplement (*Veja Rio*); *...to É* and *Carta Capital* ...r current affairs and ...onomics.

Television

...obo and *SBT* have the ...ghest viewing figures. *...obo* broadcasts the ...mous *novelas* (soaps).

EATING OUT

...azilian food is a mixture ... Portuguese, African ...d indigenous elements, ...th rice (*arroz*), black ...eans (*feijão*) and manioc ...ur (*farofa*) the staple

ingredients. Rio, the city of immigrants par excellence, offers not only regional specialties but also dishes from Portugal, Lebanon, Italy etc.

'Lanchonete'

Bar-sandwich store that serves snacks and fresh fruit juice, with a great flair for combinations like pineapple-mint and carrot-beetroot-orange. Also, *açaí na tigela*: Amazonian fruit in the form of a sorbet.

'Boteco, botequim'

Traditional café that serves hearty food, often based on Portuguese tradition: cod (*bacalhau*), squid (*lulas*), rice with broccoli.

'Churrascaria'

Restaurant serving *churrasco* from southern Brazil: buffet (*rodízio*) of salty, spit-roast meat, carved at the table.

'Comida a quilo'

Self-service. Food charged according to weight.

'Petiscos'

These snacks are designed to accompany drinks but can easily make up a meal in their own right.
Frango à passarinho: pieces of fried chicken.
Pastel: fried or baked turnovers with filling.
Empada: small meat pasty.
Bolinho de bacalhau: cod fish ball.
Aipim frito: fried manioc.
Caldinho de feijão: black-bean broth, drunk hot.
Carne seca desfiada: strips of dried meat, with boiled onions, *farofa* or fried manioc.

Culinary terms

Almoço executivo: dish of the day, served weekday lunchtime.
Batida: *cachaça* and fruit, sometimes mixed with sweetened condensed milk.
Cachaça: sugar-cane liquor.
Caipirinha: *cachaça*, lemon, sugar and crushed ice.

Also, *caipirissima* (with rum instead of *cachaça*) and caipiroska (with vodka).
Chope: draft beer.
Feijoada: Brazil's national dish, invented by the slaves and served on Saturdays. Sausages, lard, smoked meat and black beans with cabbage, oranges, *farofa* and rice.
Guaraná: fizzy drink based on the Amazonian fruit of the same name. Also available as a still drink.
Prato feito: the dish of the working classes: a full plate of fish or meat accompanied by the trio of *arroz*, *feijão* and *farofa*.

SHOWS

Circo Voador (**B** D1)

→ *Rua dos Arcos Tel. 2533-0354* Dance shows.

ATL Hall

→ *Av. Ayrton Senna, 3000 (Barra). Tel. 2430-0700*

EXCURSIONS AROUND RIO DE JANEIRO

EXCURSIONS IN THE BAY

Niterói
→ *8 miles via Rio-Niterói bridge, 20 mins by boat from the Estação das barcas*
The town on the other side of the bay: Niemeyer's Museu de Arte Contemporânea and the old fort of Santa Cruz .

Paquetá
→ *Boats from the Estação das barcas (Praça XV)*
An island with no cars.

Boat trips
→ *Thu-Sun 1.15pm, 3.15pm*
Explore the bay on a boat belonging to the Espaço cultural da Marinha (**A** E3)

ALONG THE COAST

Costa Verde
Beautiful, lush coastline to the south of Rio.
Ilha Grande
→ *Boats to Mangaratiba (90 miles via the BR101)*
Idyllic beaches, hiking.
Parati
→ *155 miles via the BR101*
A pretty colonial port once used as an outlet for the gold from Minas Gerais.
Costa do Sol
The Brazilian Riviera.
Armação dos Búzios
→ *110 miles to the east (RJ 124)*
Turquoise-water creeks in this resort popularized by Brigitte Bardot in the 60s.

LA SERRA DOS ÓRGÃOS

Petrópolis
→ *45 miles to the north (BR040)*
The Imperial Family and coffee barons used to come here to relax: palace and museum.

International stars.
Canecão (**C** E4)
→ *Av. Venceslau Brás, 215*
Tel. 2105-2000
The biggest names in Brazilian music.
Teatro Rival (**A** D4)
→ *Rua Álvaro Alvim, 33–37*
Tel. 2240-4469
The cream of MPB.

SHOPPING

Off the rack
→ *Rua Maria Quitéria* (**E** D4)
Young, sporty fashion: Osklen, Shop 126 etc.
Babilônia Feira Hype (**E** C3)
→ *Every two weeks, Sat-Sun 3–11pm; Jóquei Clube Brasileiro*
Showcase for independent designers.
Shopping malls
Rio Sul (**D** B2)
→ *Rua Lauro Muller, 116*
Central location.
Fashion Mall (**F** E2)
→ *Estrada da Gávea, 899*
Upmarket sophistication.
Downtown Shopping (**F** B2)

→ *Av. das Américas, 500*
Open-air mall, with university faculties, stores, bars and movie theaters.
Barrashopping
→ *Av. das Américas, 4666*
The biggest in Latin America.
Jewelry, luxury items
→ *Rua Garcia d'Ávila* (**E** D4)
International brand names.
Beach and surfing accessories
Galeria River (**E** F4)
→ *Rua Francisco Otaviano, 67*

RIO FROM ALL ANGLES

Favela Tours
Trips intended to demystify the city's hidden slums.
Marcelo Amstrong
→ *Tel. 3322-2727/9989-0074*
By helicopter
Helisight
→ *Tel. 2511-2141*
By boat
Cruises to see the whales and dolphins around the Cagarras Islands.

Aquabom Cruzeiros
→ *Tel. 2541-1511*

BEACHES

Postos
These numbered beacons (and landmarks) offer a lifeguard service, toilets and showers. Entrance R$2.
Types of beach
Arpoador: surfers. In front of rua Farme de Amoedo: gay. Posto 9: neo-hippy. Posto 10: yuppie. Posto 11: mothers and babies

SPORT

Hang-gliding
Launch pad on the Pedra Bonita (**F** D2).
Superfly
→ *Rui. Tel. 8123-3169*
Hiking
8,000 acres of natural park land to explore: waterfalls, excursions into the hills.
Trilharte
→ *Tel. 2556-3848*

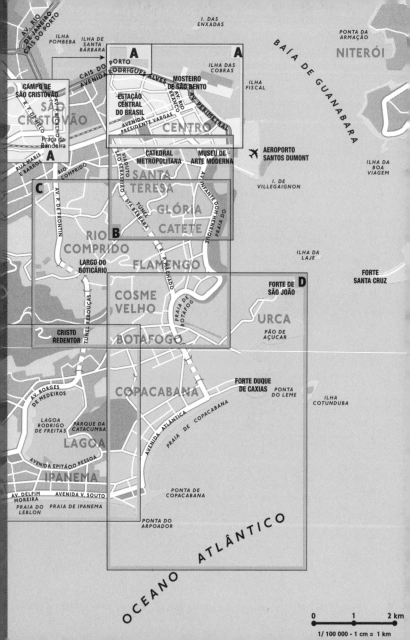

ARIA COLOMBO

TEATRO MUNICIPAL

CASA TURUNA

A conservatory with soft lighting, snug couches and cane tables is just one of several sophisticated settings for eating food based on an aromatic fusion of East and West. Top-quality jazz/bossa nova concerts Fri-Sat (10pm). Main course R$40.

TEAROOMS

Confeitaria Colombo (A D3)
→ *Rua Gonçalves Dias, 32*
Tel. 2232-2300 Mon-Sat 8am-8pm (Sat 5pm)
Superb *fin-de-siècle* tearoom (1894) – marble, stained glass, jacaranda furniture – exuding an elegance that contrasts with the hubbub of the street outside. Enjoy an ice cream or cake and imagine yourself in the Rio of years gone by.

CULTURE, DANCE, SHOWS

Cine Odéon (A D4)
→ *Praça Mahatma Gandhi, 2*
Tel. 2240-1063
The most recent (1926) of the large movie theaters flanking this square (still nicknamed 'Cinelândia') has found a new audience after a skilful restoration. Festivals, subtitled movies.

Centro Cultural Banco do Brasil (CCBB) (A D3)
→ *Rua Primeiro de Março, 60*
Tel. 3808-2020
Tue-Sun 10am-9pm
Movie screenings, plays and major exhibitions (admission free!) that are often the talk of the town. The proximity of the Casa França-Brasil, the Centro Cultural dos Corrêos and the art galleries make this district an essential cultural stopover.

Rio Scenarium (A C4)
→ *Rua do Lavradio, 20*
Tel. 3852-5516
Tue-Thu 6.30pm-2am, Fri-Sat 7pm-4am
This former antique store is now an extremely popular dance hall, set off by chandeliers, old books and display cases full of trinkets. Cocktails and dinner are also served, amidst extravagantly theatrical decor. Concerts at 6.30pm and 9.30pm.

Centro Cultural Carioca (A C3)
→ *Rua do Teatro, 37*
Tel. 2252-6468
Mon-Sat 7pm-2am
This old building, dotted with large windows, has been a famous dance hall since the 1930s. It serves as a showcase for the rising stars of samba, *choro* and *forró*.

Teatro Municipal (A D4)
→ *Praça Floriano*
Tel. 2262-3501
Guided tours: Mon-Fri 10am-5pm (every 30 mins)
This theater, based on the Paris Opera House, was opened in 1909 alongside the Rio Branco (formerly the Avenida Central). The interior is a feast of bronze, Italian marble and English glassware. Free shows on Sunday at 11am.

Gafieira Estudantina (A C4)
→ *Praça Tiradentes, 79*
Tel. 2232-1149
Thu-Sat 10.30pm-4am
For the last 70 years, elegant couples have whirled across the waxed parquet of this traditional ballroom to the rhythm of samba, bolero and tango. The orchestra performs classics from the Latin repertoire from 11pm.

Centro Luiz Gonzaga de Tradições Nordestinas (A B1)
→ *Campo de São Cristóvão*
Tel. 3860-9976
Fri 10am-Sun 11pm
Take a trip to the Brazilian northeast in this huge market, open for almost 48 hours at a stretch. Raucous musical acts, restaurants serving regional fare and craft goods.

SHOPPING

Thaisarte Artesanato (A B3)
→ *Rua Senhor dos Passos, 206. Tel. 2221-3207 Mon-Fri 9am-6pm, Sat 9am-2pm*
In the heart of the lively Saara neighborhood, straw hats, plaited beach bags, wraparound skirts and jewelry at extremely competitive prices.

Casa Turuna (A C3)
→ *Rua Senhor dos Passos, 122/124. Tel. 2509-3908 Mon-Fri 9am-7pm, Sat 8.30am-2pm*
A carnival atmosphere pervades this store throughout the year. It sells all the requisites of a female street dancer: pearls, sequins and multicolored feathers.

Casa Oliveira (A C4)
→ *Rua da Carioca, 70*
Tel. 2508-8539 Mon-Fri 9am- 7pm, Sat 9am-1pm
All the percussion instruments used by the *bateria* of a samba school are on show here: *surdo, cuíca, pandeiro, repique...*

Lidador (A C3)
→ *Rua da Assembléia, 65*
Tel. 2533-4988 Mon-Fri 9am-7.30pm, Sat 9am-2pm
Sophisticated Portuguese grocery store (1924). Wide range of Portuguese, Chilean and Argentinian wines.

ABINETE PORTUGUÊS DE LEITURA

IGREJA SÃO FRANCISCO DA PENITÊNCIA

D   E   F

DE GUANABARA

1

MOSTEIRO DE
SÃO BENTO
★

UA DOM
ERARDO

R. SARAIVA
RUA VISC.
ITABORAÍ

BECO DE
BRAGANÇA

OTONI

NOSSA SENHORA
DA CANDELÁRIA

CASA
FRANÇA-
BRASIL
CCBB

ILHA DAS
COBRAS

ILHA FISCAL ★

2

CAIS DO
PHAROUX

TRAVESSA DO
COMÉRCIO

RGAS   Praça
Pio X

AV. PRES. KUBITSCHEK

R. I. DE MARÇO

AV. PRES.

PAQUETÁ
NITERÓI

ESPAÇO CULTURAL
DA MARINHA

N.S. DA LAPA
MERCADORES

BUENOS AIRES
R. DA ALFÂNDEGA
R. DO ROSÁRIO
R. DO OUVIDOR

ESTAÇÃO
DAS BARCAS

N.S. DO
CARMO

PRAÇA QUINZE
★

R. DO QUITAN

N.S. DO
MONTE   Praça XV

KU

3

AV. RIO BRAN

IANA

Map fragment showing streets including RUA 7 DE SETEMBRO, RUA DA ASSE..., AVENIDA RES. A CARLOS, AV. NILO PEÇANHA, PALÁCIO DA JUSTIÇA (FORUM), MUSEU DA IMAGEM E DO SOM, MISERICÓRDIA, Praça Barbosa, LARGO DA CARIOCA, CARIOCA, MUSEU NACIONAL DE BELAS ARTES, RUA A. BARROSO, RUA DEBRET, PALÁCIO GUSTAVO CAPANEMA, RUA M. AGUINALDO, MUSEU HISTÓRICO NACIONAL, AEROPORTO SANTOS DUMONT, SANTA CASA DE MISERICÓRDIA, TEATRO MUNICIPAL, Praça Floriano Peixoto, CINELÂNDIA, AV. G. ARANHA, RUA DA IMPRENSA, R. S. LUZIA, AV. MARECHAL CÂMARA, AV. GENERAL JUSTO, RUA A. PORTO ALEGRE, CINELÂNDIA, RUA MÉXICO, AV. CHURCHILL, AV. WILSON, AV. PRES. WILSON, AV. ROOSEVELT, Praça M. Gandhi, Praça Itália, Praça Senador Salgado Filho, R. S. CHURCHILL, scale 0 – 125 – 250 m

HISTÓRICO NACIONAL

MARACANÃ

QUINTA DA BOA VISTA

sual records of the
World, painted by the
man Frans Post (1612–
d 20 works by Boudin.
vento de
Antônio /
São Francisco da
ência (A D4)
o da Carioca
i 9am–noon, 1–4pm
plex made up of a
nt (1780) and two
es (1608–20). The
of the church of São
sco da Penitência
–1736) conceals one
great treasures of
an baroque, with
pe-l'oeil ceiling,
fed *talha* (wooden
ure) and a
ficent altarpiece in

the axial chapel.
★ Palácio Gustavo
Capanema (A E4)
→ *Rua da Imprensa, 16*
Office hours
The former Ministry of
Education, a landmark in
modern architecture, was
put up between 1937 and
1943 by a team of architects
led by Oscar Niemeyer (and
advised by Le Corbusier).
The sun shields and 33-foot-
high pilotis (flanked by tiles
designed by Di Calvacanti)
caused a sensation in
their day.
★ Museu Histórico
Nacional (A F3)
→ *Praça Marechal Âncora*
Tel. 2550-9220 Tue-Fri 10am–
5.30pm, Sat-Sun 2–6pm

The National Historical
Museum is housed in the
old fort of Santiago (17th c.),
formerly on the waterfront,
in the front line of the bay's
defenses. The story of
Brazil from 1500 to 1889:
furniture, paintings,
documents etc.
★ Maracanã (A A1)
→ *Rua Professor Eurico*
Rabelo Tel. 2568-9962
When this stadium was
completed in 1950, it was
the biggest in the world,
and it was here, in 1969,
that Pelé scored the
thousandth goal of his
career. It is the venue for
matches between the city's
four main soccer clubs (but
the crowds are as much of

a spectacle as the players).
Small sports museum.
★ Quinta
da Boa Vista (A A1)
→ *Av. Pedro II, between*
Ruas Almirante Baltazar and
Dom Meinrado.
Museu Nacional:
Tue-Sun 10am–4pm.
Jardim Zoológico (Rua Catalão)
Tue-Sun 9am–4.30pm
This neoclassical palace
served as the residence for
first the royal family, then
the imperial family. The
romantic gardens were
created in 1869 and the
National Museum was
installed after the fall of the
Empire (natural history,
archeology, anthropology).
The park contains Rio's zoo.

A

B

C

MUSEU DA CHÁCARA DO CÉU

MUSEU DO BONDE

IGREJA NOSSA SENHORA DA GLÓRIA DO OU

★ **Sambódromo** (B A2)
→ *Rua Marquês de Sapucaí*
The Sambódromo (1984)
is the stage for Rio's
carnival, the world's
biggest party, famous for
its explosion of floats and
dancing girls adorned with
feathers and sequins. In
his quest for a setting that
matched the extravagance
of the event, Oscar
Niemeyer came up with
a street half a mile long,
flanked by bleachers with
a capacity of over 70,000
spectators, who all come
to see the parade of the
samba schools from the
grupo especial (the best
14 in Rio).

★ **Catedral
Metropolitana** (B D1)
→ *Av. República do Chile, 245
Daily 7am–7pm Masses:
Mon–Fri 11am, Sat–Sun 10am*
This unusual cathedral –
a cut-off pyramid designed
by Edgar Fonseca and
finished in 1979 – can hold
up to 20,000 people. The
stained-glass windows soar
upward for over 300 feet!
A translucent cross on the
top, centered within a circle
100 feet in diameter,
symbolizes the presence
of Christ among men.
Museu do Bonde (B C3)
→ *Rua Carlos Brant, 14
Tel. 2242-2354
Daily 9am–4.30pm*

A small tram museum with
more than 300 exhibits
illustrating the history
of transportation, from
horse-drawn carriages to
British equipment from
the late 19th century.
★ **Escadaria
Selarón** (B D2)
→ *Escadaria Manuel Carneiro*
One of the landmarks of
Santa Teresa: 215 steps
covered with tiles in the
colors of the Brazilian flag
lead up to the Carmelite
convent. Conceived as a
tribute to the Brazilian
people, it is a labor of love
for the indefatigable Chilean
artist Selarón, who has
never ceased to make

adjustments since sta
work in 1990.
★ **Museu da Cháca**
do Céu / Parque
das Ruínas (B C2)
→ *Rua Murtinho Nobre
Tel. 2507-1932 Museum
Wed–Mon noon–5pm;
Park: Tue–Sun 10am–8p*
An exquisite Moderni
built by Wladimir Alve
Souza is the showcas
the superb collection
pineapple magnate C
Maya (1894–1968): pa
from Brazil and Europ
(Portinari, Dalí), deco
art and watercolors b
Baptiste Debret chron
the city's life in the ea
19th century. The nea

SAMBÓDROMO

CATEDRAL METROPOLITANA

Map labels:

A B C

VIADUTO SÃO SEBASTIÃO
RUA MQ. DE POMBAL
RUA DE SANTANA
RUA GEN. CALDWELL
M. FILHO
CAMPO DE SANTANA
RUA VISC. DO
AV. G
SE
FREIRE
Praça da República
RUA FREI CANECA
RUA 20 DE ABRIL
R. D. INVALIDOS
R. U. DO
AV. REP
AV. MEM DE SÁ
R. DO SENADO
RUA
RUA DOS INVALIDOS
RUA
R. MARQUES DE SAPUCAI
RUA DO
Praça Cruz Vermelha
★ SAMBÓDROMO
RUA PAULA MATOS
AV. HENRIQUE VALADARES
RIACHUELO
RUA W.
R. C. SAMPAIO
LUIS
AMARAL
RESENDE
RUA DO
AVENIDA MEM
RUA DO CATUMBI
RUA C. REIDNER
VIA ELEVADA
R. J DE ALENCAR
RUA DO PARAISO
R. P. MATOS
R. FLUMINENSE
RUA E. SANTOS
RUA COSTA BASTOS
AV. N.S. DE
R. M. ALEGRE
RUA DO RIACHUE
RUA ANDRE CASTRO
LADEIRA DO CASTRO
RUA
2
RUA PROGRESSO
R. CARDEAL D. SEBASTIÃO
MUSEU D CHÁCARA DO
PARQUE RUI
CEMITÉRIO DO CATUMBI
LARGO DAS NEVES
R. PE. MIGUELINHO
RUA DO ORIENTE
RUA MONTE ALEGRE
LADEIRA D. SEBASTIÃO LEME
RUA ITAPIRU
R. E. DE ALMEIDA
R. V. ALEGRE
R. ENG. M. AUSTREGESILO
RUA TERESÓPOLIS
RUA CARLOS BRANDT
R. ALMIRAN
R. DR. AGRA
RUA GONÇALVES
RUA
★ MUSEU
3

Lapa comes alive at night, when revelers of all types jam into its bars and clubs until the early hours. This is a new phenomenon for this once maligned neighborhood, formerly the domain of prostitutes and other colorful characters (although this seediness always attracted thrill seekers from more respectable areas!). The aqueduct lined with rails cleaves the sky to link up with Santa Teresa, leaving the tram to wind through alleyways reminiscent of a small town, much loved by hirsute artists and intellectuals. To the east, the land reclaimed from the sea has been used to create an impressive park on the edge of the bay, set off by the small church of Glória.

BAR DO ARNAUDO

APRAZÍVEL

RESTAURANTS

Bar do Arnaudo (A C3)
→ Rua Almirante Alexandrino, 316
Tel. 2252-7246
Daily noon–11pm
(7pm Mon; 8pm Sat-Sun)
The food here is rooted in the arid lands of the northeastern interior: huge portions of *jaba com jerimum* (dried meat with pumpkin), sweet potatoes, *farofa* and *feijão de corda* (a type of bean). A tram stops outside the door. Main course R$25 (for two).

Bar do Mineiro (A B3)
→ Rua Paschoal Carlos Magno, 99. Tel. 2221-9227
Daily 11am–2pm
(4am Fri-Sat; 7pm Sun)
This authentic *boteco* has long been a favorite with the locals, particularly for the *feijoada* served at the weekend. Specialties from Minas are also available: *frango com quiabo* (chicken with okra) and homemade black-bean *pasteis*. Set menu R$15.

Sobrenatural (A C3)
→ Rua Almirante Alexandrino, 432
Tel. 2224-1003
Daily noon–midnight
This pretty old *sobrado*, close to the Largo dos Guimarães, offers food from the coast of Bahia,

seasoned with fresh coriander, palm oil and coconut milk: *moqueca de peixe* (fish stew), *bobó de camarão* (shrimps with mashed manioc). Main course R$22.

Nova Capela (A D2)
→ Av. Mem de Sá, 96
Tel. 2508-8493
Daily 11am–5am
This is the perfect place to while away the night and watch the comings and goings of the Lapa's bohemian set. The house specialty, *cabrito* (kid), is served with rice and broccoli. Main course R$42 (for two).

Taberna do Juca (A D2)
→ Av. Mem de Sá, 65
Tel. 2221-9839
Daily noon–3am
In the warm atmosphere of the Avenida Mem de Sá, this Portuguese restaurant that serves mainly squid, cod and other fish dishes, provides a good starting point for a night on the town – or a snack of kid broth and cornbread later on. Set menu R$35–40.

Aprazível (A B4)
→ Rua Aprazível, 62
Tel. 2508-9174 Thu-Sat noon–midnight, Sun 1–7pm
The tables of this bucolic hideaway on the heights

CA DA GEMA   FUNDIÇÃO PROGRESSO   LARGO DAS LETRAS

of Santa Teresa are laid out under enormous mango, guava and avocado trees, and have stunning views of the Guanabara Bay. The inventive dishes include grilled fish with orange juice, coconut rice and plantain. Live *chorinho* orchestra (small guitar, flute and tambourine) on Thursday nights. Set menu R$60.

Barracuda (A F3)
→ *Marina da Glória (Aterro do Flamengo)*
Tel. 2265-4641
Mon-Sat noon–midnight,
Sun noon–6pm
Smoked-glass windows provide a cozy setting for sampling superbly fresh seafood in front of the boats on the Marina da Glória. Try the T*ridente de coisas do mar* (a platter of grilled prawns, lobster, squid and fish). Main course R$60–80.

BARS, MUSIC

Goyabeira (A B2)
→ *Largo das Neves, 13*
Tel. 2232-5751 Daily 6pm–midnight (2am Fri-Sat)
This unpretentious bar on a small square bounded by a tramline serves delicious honey and coconut *batidas*,

accompanied by fried manioc, grilled sausages and prawn fritters.
Simplesmente (A B3)
→ *Rua Paschoal Carlos Magno, 115. Tel. 2508-6007*
Mon-Sat 6pm–4am
A tiny but lively bar, popular with young people. It quickly fills up on concert nights (samba and *choro*, Wednesday).
Clube dos Democráticos (A C2)
→ *Rua do Riachuelo, 91-93*
Tel. 2252-4611
Thu-Sat 10pm
The HQ of one of Rio's oldest samba clubs (1867) boasts a huge ballroom reached via a beautiful staircase, and provides a chance to enjoy time-honored dances in a lively atmosphere.
Teatro Odisséia (A D2)
→ *Av. Mem de Sá, 66*
Tel. 2507-8432
The characteristics of the urban tribe thronging the door vary according to the program on offer. Electronic music and parties masterminded by DJs.
Carioca da Gema (A D2)
→ *Av. Mem de Sá, 79*
Tel. 2221-0043
Mon-Fri 6pm–2am (4am Fri), Sat 9pm–4am
From 10pm onward, this music bar offers the city's

best samba and *choro* groups (including rising young stars). It gets very crowded, so arrive early to avoid waiting in line.
Fundição Progresso (A D1)
→ *Rua dos Arcos, 24-50*
Tel. 2220-5070
This multipurpose arts center alongside the Lapa Arches plays host to circus workshops and theater groups, while its concerts attract young people from all of Rio's southern neighborhoods.

SHOPPING

Largo das Letras (A C3)
→ *Rua Almirante Alexandrina, 501*
Tel. 2221-8992 Tue-Sat 2–10pm, Sun 2–8pm
In the midst of lush mango and banana trees, this 19th-century villa overlooking the Largo dos Guimarães houses a delightful bookstore-cum-café. Ideal for a short break.
La Vereda (A C3)
→ *Rua Almirante Alexandrina, 428*
Tel. 2507-0317
Daily 10am–9pm
This pretty store displays the work of painters from Santa Teresa (sometimes known as 'Rio's

Montmartre'), as well as pottery, embroidery and craft goods incorporating recycled materials (drapes made of metal can tops).
Brechó Arte 70 (A B3)
→ *Rua Monte Alegre, 337*
Tel. 2221-3205
Mon-Sat 10.30am–9pm (7pm Mon), Sun 2–9pm
The second-hand clothes from the 1970s on sale here (floral skirts, plastic accessories) have acquired a cult following among the young women of the neighborhood.
Novo Desenho (A F2)
→ *Av. Infante Dom Henrique, 85 (Museum of Modern Art)*
Tel. 2524-2290 Tue-Sun noon–6pm (7pm Sat-Sun)
Everything here is the work of a top Brazilian designer (Lina Bo Bardi, Guto, Indio da Bahia, Mauricio Klabin), from the furniture to the smallest accessory.
From R$6 to R$4,000!
Feira da Glória (A E2)
→ *Av. Augusto Severo*
Mon-Fri 9am–7.30pm,
Sat 9am–2pm
Shopping in the picturesque Glória market is an experience that involves strolling past piles of chillis and medicinal roots to the syncopated rhythms of the group Cazinha Carioca.

ORAL METROPOLITANA

ARCOS DA LAPA

ESCADARIA SELARÓN

D

IGREJA DE
SÃO FRANCISCO
DA PENITÊNCIA

CARIOCA

AVENIDA ALM. BARROSO

SANTA CASA
DE MISERICÓRDIA

F NOSSA
SENHORA DO
BOMSUCESSO

CONVENTO
SANTO ANTÔNIO

R. LÉLIO
GAMA

TEATRO
MUNICIPAL

MUSEU
NACIONAL DE
BELAS ARTES

AVENIDA
CHURCHILL

CHILE

Praça
Floriano
Peixoto

PALÁCIO
GUSTAVO
CAPANEMA

ESTAÇÃO
DE BONDES

CINELÂNDIA

CATEDRAL
TROPOLITANA

R. PEDRO LESSA

AVENIDA
ROOSEVELT

R. ÁLVARO ALVIM

CINELÂNDIA

Praça
Francisco
Pinto

MÉXICO

Praça
Italia

DOS ARCOS

Praça
Mahatma
Gandhi

ARCOS
DA LAPA

RUA DO PASSEIO

RUA JARDEL JERCOLIS

APA

PASSEIO
PÚBLICO

Largo da
Lapa

TEIXEIRA
DE FREITAS

Praça
Deodoro

MUSEU DE
ARTE MODERNA

PARQUE DO
FLAMENGO

2

RTINHO

RUA M.
CANEIRO

RUA DA LAPA

ESCADARIA
SELARÓN

R. AUGUSTO SEVERO

Praça
Paris

MONUMENTO
AOS MORTOS DA
2a GUERRA MUNDIAL

ENSEADA
DA GLÓRIA

ROS

AVENIDA BEIRA MAR

PARQUE DO
FLAMENGO

ESA

R. R. M.
EBRÃO

Praça
Paris

R. DA GLÓRIA

RUA CÂNDIDO MENDES

GLÓRIA

IGREJA
NOSSA SENHORA
DA GLÓRIA

MARINA DA
GLÓRIA

CONSTANT

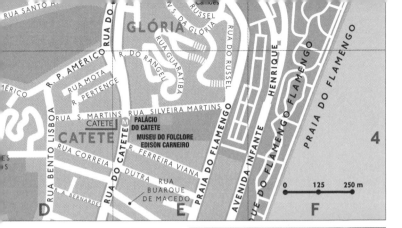

GLÓRIA

RUA SANTO A...

R. P. AMÉRICO
R. DO RANGEL
RUA GUARATIBA
N.S. DA GLÓRIA
RUSSEL
Camões
RUA DA GLÓRIA
RUA DO RUSSEL
RUA MOTA
R. PERTENCE
RUA S. MARTINS
RUA SILVEIRA MARTINS
CATETE
PALÁCIO DO CATETE
MUSEU DO FOLCLORE EDISÓN CARNEIRO
RUA BENTO LISBOA
RUA CORREIA
R. FERREIRA VIANA
RUA BUARQUE DE MACEDO
A. BERNARDES
RUA DUTRA
RUA DO CATETE
AVENIDA INFANTE
RUA DO FLAMENGO
PRAIA DO FLAMENGO
HENRIQUE
FLAMENGO
PRAIA DO FLAMENGO

4

0   125   250 m

D   E   F

...JE DO FLAMENGO

MUSEU DE ARTE MODERNA / MAM

of Ruins contains the ...ins of the villa of the ...st and artistic patron ...nda Santos Lobo, as ...s providing an ...otional view of the bay.

:cos da Lapa (B D2) *...m terminus (Estação ...ndes): Rua Lélio Gama ...42-2354 ...ic tour: Sat 10am, 2pm* ...d between the hills of ...a Teresa and Santo ...io, the 18th-century ...r went on to be used ...e old Santa Teresa ...ine in 1877. Part of the ...has been maintained

in two sections. Get off at either Curvelo or Largo dos Guimarães to explore the hilltop neighborhood of Santa Teresa.

★ **Parque do Flamengo (B** E2)
This park, designed by Roberto Burle Marx, was built in the 1960s on land reclaimed from the sea; it spans 50 acres, running from the airport to Botafogo Bay! Its rich vegetation is enticing at any time, but it is best seen on Sundays, when the park is closed to traffic. Toward the northern end stands a striking Modernist monument to the victims of World War 2.

★ **Museu de Arte Moderna / MAM (B** F2)
→ *Av. Infante Dom Henrique, 85. Tel. 2240-4944 Tue-Fri noon–6pm, Sat-Sun noon–7pm*
This is undoubtedly the most daring building created by Alfonso Reidy (1958), as it rests on concrete arches. All around, the gardens designed by Burle Marx alternate mineral compositions, palm trees and rolling lawns. A fire destroyed most of the museum's contents in 1978, but it has since acquired the collection of Gilberto Chateaubriand, a tenacious champion of contemporary

art, with conceptual works by the likes of Hélio Oiticica and Cildo Meireles. Temporary exhibitions.

★ **Igreja Nossa Senhora da Glória do Outeiro (B** E3)
→ *Access via funicular train from Rua do Russel, 312 Tel. 2225-2869 Mon-Fri 8am–5pm, Sat-Sun 8am–noon*
This exquisite baroque church (1739), laid out in the form of two octagons, stands on top of a small hill with an enchanting view of the Parque do Flamengo. Its sculpted decor, somewhere between rococo and neoclassical, is set off by magnificent tiles. It's also a sacred art museum.

CRISTO REDENTOR

CRISTO REDENTOR

MUSEU DE ARTE NAÏF (MIA

★ Museu da República (C F1)

→ Rua do Catete, 153
Tel. 2558-6350 Tue-Fri
noon–5pm, Sat-Sun 2–6pm
The former presidential palace (originally the mansion of a coffee baron) is the appropriate setting for the Museum of the Republic, which offers a lively survey of the decisive moments in Brazilian history. The room in which the populist president Getúlio Vargas (1883–1954), committed suicide in response to overwhelming dissent has been left intact. Its last occupant, Juscelino Kubitschek, left the palace

in 1960 in favor of the new capital, Brasilia. Be sure to take a stroll around the large English-style park, with its impressive avenue of palm trees.

★ Museu do Folclore Edison Carneiro (C F1)

→ Rua do Catete, 179, 181
Tel. 2285-0441 Tue-Fri
11am–6pm, Sat-Sun 3–6pm
This collection of over 1,500 objects reveals the vitality and richness of Brazilian popular art via five different sections: life, technique, religion, festival and art. Particularly striking are the painted figurines of Mestre Vitalino (1909–63), from the State of Pernambouc,

and his disciples Manuel Eudócio and Zé Cabocio, as well as the work of artists from the Vale do Jequitinhonha (Minas Gerais) like the brilliant potter Ulisses Pereira Chaves (b. 1922).

★ Sesc Flamengo (C E2)

→ Rua Marquês de Abrantes, 99
Tel. 3138-1343 Tue-Sat
noon–8pm, Sun 11am–5pm;
classical music on Sat at 5pm;
movie club on Sun at 5pm
Tucked between the houses of the Flamengo district, the curving forms of the white Villa Figner bear witness to the eclectic taste of Rio's middle class in the early

20th century. Now a cu
center with art gallerie
a restaurant. Interestin
program of free events
(visual art, music, mov

★ Parque Guinle (C

Overlooking gardens i
form of an amphithea
the neoclassical Palác
Laranjeiras built by An
Carlos da Silva Telles,
now the residence of t
Governor of the State
Rio. The park is flanke
a fine set of Modernist
houses (1948–54),
designed by Lúcio Cos
Their brick latticework
covered with mosaics
reveals the influence c
popular architecture.

C

MUSEU DA REPÚBLICA

MUSEU DA REPÚBLICA

MUSEU DO FOLCLORE EDISON CARNEIRO

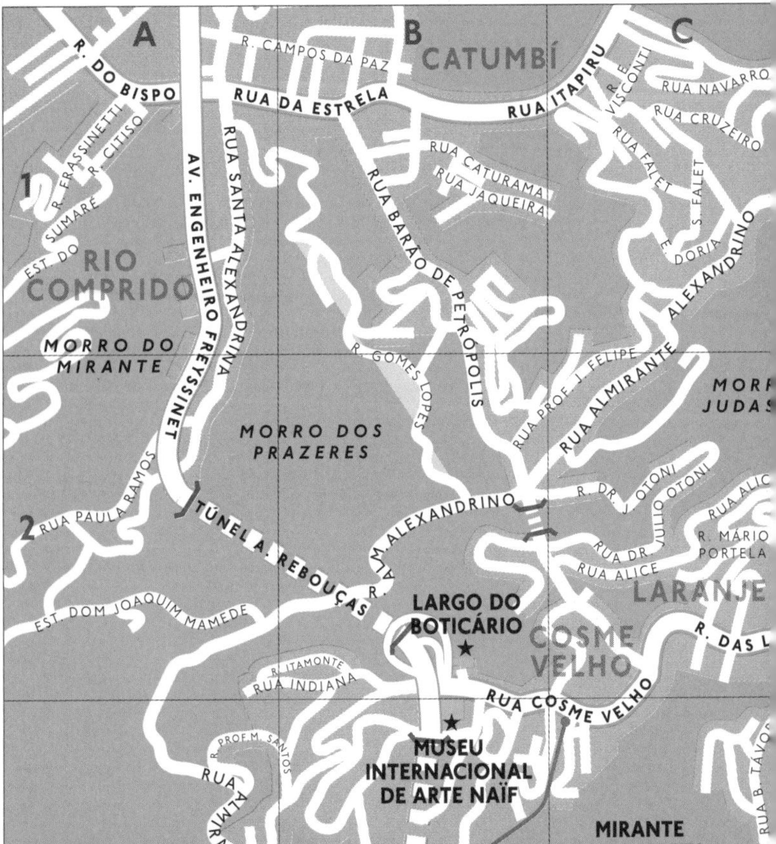

A

B — CATUMBÍ

C

R. DO BISPO

R. CAMPOS DA PAZ

RUA DA ESTRELA

RUA ITAPIRU

R. FRASSINETTI

R. CITISO

EST. DO SUMARÉ

RUA SANTA ALEXANDRINA

AV. ENGENHEIRO FREYSSINET

RUA CATURAMA

RUA JAQUEIRA

RUA BARÃO DE PETRÓPOLIS

R. VISCONTI

RUA NAVARRO

RUA CRUZEIRO

RUA FALET

S. FALET

DORIA

E. ALEXANDRINO

1

RIO COMPRIDO

MORRO DO MIRANTE

MORRO DOS PRAZERES

R. GOMES LOPES

RUA PROF. J. FELIPE

RUA ALMIRANTE

MORR JUDAS

TÚNEL A. REBOUÇAS

RUA PAULA RAMOS

AV. M. ALEXANDRINO

R. DR. J. OTONI

JULIO OTONI

RUA ALIC

R. MÁRIO PORTELA

2

EST. DOM JOAQUIM MAMEDE

R. ALEXANDRINO

RUA DR

RUA ALICE

LARANJE

LARGO DO BOTICÁRIO ★

COSME VELHO

R. DAS L

R. ITAMONTE

RUA INDIANA

RUA COSME VELHO

R. PROF. M. SANTOS

MUSEU INTERNACIONAL DE ARTE NAÏF ★

RUA

RUA B. TAVOR

3

MIRANTE DONA MARTA

An invigorating hubbub reigns on Rua do Catete, a popular shopping street lined with dilapidated *sobrados* (two-story buildings). Only the old Presidential Palace bears witness to the area's past glories. Largo do Machado, a leafy square where old men meet to play cards or chess, marks the border of Laranjeiras, with its schools and neighborhood stores. This district follows the valley of the Carioca River to Cosme Velho, coiled at the feet of Christ the Redeemer. On the edge of the bay, Flamengo has two faces: freeways and opulent residences on the Aterro side; restaurants, bars and more humble accommodation away from the shoreline.

MERCADO SÃO JOSÉ

SEVERYNA

RESTAURANTS

Adega Portugália (C E1)
→ *Largo do Machado, 30-A*
Tel. 2558-2821
Daily 10.30am–2am
Authentic Portuguese food served behind the square of the Largo do Machado, in such large portions that budget-conscious travelers can easily share a dish between two or three: *ula* (squid), *bacalhau* (cod) and other fish.
À la carte R$25.

Estação República (C E1)
→ *Rua do Catete, 104*
Tel. 2225-2650
Daily 11am–midnight
One of the neighborhood's best *comida a quilo* joints, with a meticulous decor. Salads, fried vegetables, fritters and succulent meat from the grill in the back. 100 g (3 ½ oz) for R$2.50 (meal approx. R$15).

Lamas (C E2)
→ *Rua Marquês de Abrantes, 18-A. Tel. 2556-0799*
Daily 7.30am–3am
The building may not be the same as the Lamas that opened in 1874, but the magic remains and the customers still include a sprinkling of politicians, artists and students. In fact, the atmosphere is everything here, as the cooking and setting

are surprisingly simple. Very generous portions. Main course R$30.

Mercado São José (C E2)
→ *Rua das Laranjeiras, 90*
Tel. 2557-0202 Tue-Fri 4pm–1am (2.30am Fri), Sat-Sun noon–2am (midnight Sun)
A market from the 1940s with five restaurants and five different types of regional cooking. Tables are set outside in the old courtyard, where a constant, joyous noise pervades. Main course R$20.

Severyna (C E2)
→ *Rua Ipiranga, 54*
Tel. 2556-9398
Daily 11.30am–1am
Severyna is as popular for its nighttime atmosphere as for its food, with echoes of the *Sertão* (the northeastern scrubland). The *xaxado* – a platter of dried meat, manioc, *queijo coalho* (cheese made with melted curds) for two or three people – is ideal for concert nights. Music daily 9pm (*forró* evenings on Monday). Participation in the music R$8–10. À la carte R$20.

Porcão Rio's (C F2)
→ *Av. Infante Dom Henrique (Aterro do Flamengo)*
Tel. 3461-9020
Daily 11.30am–midnight (1am Fri-Sat)

E JUAQUIM   MARACATU BRASIL   BRUMADO

This is undoubtedly the most famous of all Rio's *churrascarias*; its glass dining room looks out onto a picture-postcard landscape, with the bay and the Sugarloaf Mountain in the foreground. Reserve to make sure of a good view. *Rodízio* (buffet) R$54.

Tasca do Edgar (C D2)
→ *Rua Alice, 21*
Tel. 2558-9447
Tue-Sun 11am–3am
If you want to try the traditional *eão Veloso* soup (fish and seafood) in a peaceful atmosphere, come in the daytime. At night, things hot up as the late-night party people pass by before going to Casa Rosa, a little further uphill. Main course R$25.

CAFÉS, BARS

Belmonte (C F2)
→ *Praia do Flamengo, 300*
Tel. 2507-6873
Daily 6am–3am
Here, all the action takes place outside the bar, and the waiters, distinguished by their aprons, go out on the sidewalk to take orders from customers leaning nonchalantly against the hoods of cars! They drink standing up, talk loudly and block the traffic until

the early hours.
Tacacá do Norte (C E2)
→ *Rua Barão do Flamengo, 35.* Tel. 2205-7545
Daily 9am–10pm
Take a trip to the State of Pará by sipping Amazonian juices with mysterious names (*bacuri, cupuaçú, taperebá*). Adventurous souls can try the *tacacá*, a thick Indian broth with manioc, dried prawns and *jambú* (the leaves of a plant that slightly inflame the lips and tongue).
Manoel e Juaquim (C E2)
→ *Rua Almirante de Tamandaré, 77*
Tel. 2556-7385 *Tue-Sat 5pm–2am, Sun 1pm–2am*
The small can of olive oil on each table encourages customers to try the snacks: cod fritters and other classics of the *botequim*. Tuesdays are devoted to specialties based on *siri* (small white crab) – in stews and soups, gratinéed etc.
Bistrô Jardins (C F1)
→ *Rua do Catete, 153*
Tel. 2558-2673
Mon-Fri 9.30am–6pm,
Sat-Sun 9am–6pm
A few white, wrought-iron tables are set amidst century-old trees in the gardens of the Palácio da República. Breakfasts, espressos, pies, salads.

MUSIC, DANCE

Clan Café (C C2)
→ *Rua Cosme Velho, 564*
Tel. 2558-2322
Tue-Sat 6pm–3am
Behind the front room of this pretty café, the terrace serves as a stage for groups playing jazz, blues and MPB (*Musica Popular Brasileira*). Good selection of cocktails (Sex on the Beach, Kamikaze, Bloody Mary); music daily at 9pm (*chorinho* on Tuesdays).
Casa Rosa (C C2)
→ *Rua Alice, 550*
Tel. 9363-4645 *Fri-Sat 11pm– 5am, Sun 7pm–2am*
In the largely residential Rua Alice, a villa serves as one of Rio's last brothels. This is the place for a wild night on the town, with none of the discretion of years gone by. Garden and a variety of settings; the program includes live performances of samba, *forró*, reggae.

SHOPPING

Grão Integral (C E2)
→ *Rua das Laranjeiras, 43 Loja 12.* Tel. 2285-6739
Mon-Fri 8am–7.30pm,
Sat 7am–6pm
Essential oils, medicinal infusions, ground

guaraná, honey, propolis and a host of flours and powders with beneficial effects. The store also serves *comida a quilo*.
Maracatu Brasil (C E2)
→ *Rua Ipiranga, 49*
Tel. 2557-4754 *Mon-Fri 10am–6pm, Sat 10am–2pm*
This Mecca for lovers of percussion has an international reputation. On the ground floor is a store selling Brazilian percussion instruments; upstairs are workshops (samba, *maracatu, candomblé* etc.) led by the master musicians.
Pé de Boi (C E2)
→ *Rua Ipiranga, 55*
Tel. 2285-4395 *Mon-Fri 9am–7pm, Sat 9am–1pm*
One of the standard bearers of Brazilian handicrafts. Terracotta dolls from the Vale de Jequitinhonha (Minas Gerais), statuettes from the Alto do Moura (Pernambuco), Indian baskets, woodcuts etc.
Brumado (C C2)
→ *Rua das Laranjeiras, 486-B.* Tel. 2558-2275
Mon-Fri 9am–7pm,
Sat 10am–2pm
On your way to the Corcovado station, make sure you drop by this enchanting craft store: furniture, decorative objects, sculpture etc.

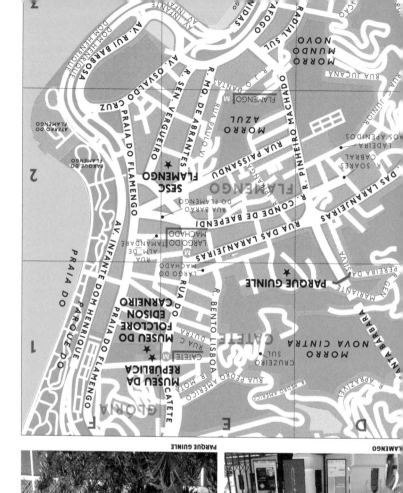

↓ Map B

PARQUE GUINLE

FLAMENGO

DO BOTICÁRIO

MIRANTE DONA MARTA

sto Redentor (C A4)
*n do Corcovado
sme Velho, 513
58-1329
ures daily 8.30am–
n, every 30 mins;
ute ride*
mbol of Rio, the
c statue of Christ
deemer on top of the
ado Mountain,
ts the city with its
etched arms. It can
ched by road or rack
y (1884); either way,
cent of no less than
feet will take you
h the lush Tijuca
The summit offers
htaking 360° view
city, the hills and

the sea; onlookers are
further dwarfed by the
27-foot-high pedestal and
100-foot concrete statue
(1932), designed by Heitor
da Silva Costa and Carlos
Oswaldo, and partially
sculpted by the Frenchman
Paul Landowski (head
and hands).

★ **Museu Internacional
de Arte Naïf (MIAN)** **(C** B3)
→ *Rua Cosme Velho, 561
Tel. 2205-8612
Tue-Fri 10am–6pm,
Sat-Sun noon–6pm*
Set in a 19th-century
bourgeois house with a
large garden dotted with
ancient mango trees, the
MIAN contains one of the

world's largest collections
of naive art, with Brazilian
painters obviously taking
pride of place: there are
scenes from everyday life
and Bahian women in
multicolored costumes.

★ **Largo
do Boticário (C** B2)
→ *Rua Cosme Velho, 822*
A small corner of old-style
Rio was preserved here in
the 1940s, in reaction to
the large-scale demolition
caused by the construction
of the Avenida Presidente
Vargas. The quiet little
square, surrounded by
pastel-colored houses,
almost has a village feel –
only enhanced by the

sound of the Carioca River
flowing nearby.

★ **Mirante
Dona Marta (C** C3)
→ *Estrada do Mirante Dona
Marta (take Estr. do
Corcovado, then Estr. dos
Paineiras). Daily 9am–6pm*
This belvedere, perched
1,100 feet up, in the midst
of the Tijuca Forest,
provides one of Rio's most
famous vantage points,
taking in almost the entire
city from the Rio-Niterói
bridge to the
neighborhoods opened
up to the Atlantic. The
nearby heliport also offers
views of the lagoon and
the Corcovado.

URCA

PÃO DE AÇÚCAR

(map labels)

RUA ULRICH
RUA ALMIRANTE GONÇALVES
POSTO 5
RUA SÁ FERREIRA
RUA PROF. SÁ
AV. N. S. COPACABANA
R. POMPÉIA
POSTO 6 **FORTE DE COPACABANA**
R. J. NABUCO
RUA F. OTAVIANO
Praça Cel. Eugênio Franco
BAÍA DO DIABO
PARQUE GAROTA DE IPANEMA

PEDRA DO ARPOADOR

OCEAN

0 250 500 m

A   B

5

6

★ **Urca** (**D** C2)
→ *Bus 107 (Central-Urca), 511 or 512 (Leblon-Urca)*
This pretty peninsula's abandoned casino endows it with a faded charm.
The tip is one of the most pleasant spots in the whole of Rio, with narrow streets flanked by low, early-20th-century houses.
Neoclassical architecture abounds on the Avenida Pasteur, while styles from the 1930s dominate Ruas Urbano Santos and Otávio Correia. Continuing round the bay, you will pass a line of fishing rods attended by their patient owners before reaching the Cuadrado da Urca, a sleepy harbor with brightly colored little boats bobbing on the water. Stunning views and all the calm of a provincial town.

★ **Museu Casa de Rui Barbosa** (**D** A2)
→ *Rua São Clemente, 134 Tel. 2537-0036 Tue-Fri 9am–5pm, Sat-Sun 2–6pm*
This huge house (1849) was the residence of the jurist Rui Barbosa (1849–1923), a prolific writer whose complete works amount to 137 volumes! It exudes the atmosphere of Rio's intellectual circles in the early days of the Republic (whose Constitution was drawn up in 1891 by Rui Barbosa himself, a fervent abolitionist and democrat).

★ **Pão de Açúcar** (**D** D2) (**Sugarloaf Mountain**)
→ *Av. Pasteur, 520 Tel. 2546-8400 Daily 8.10am–10pm. Cable car every 30 mins from Praia Vermelha*
The Sugarloaf Mountain, on the edge of the Atlantic, has provided Rio with its favorite postcard image. The ascent by cable car is divided into two parts: a stopover at the Morro de Urca, before heading off again over a dizzying void. The 1,295-foot peak affords a magnificent 360° view of the beaches of Flamengo, Copacabana, Leme, Ipanema and Leblon, as well as the flat sum Gávea, the Corvocado and, at the back of the the Serra do Mar, with 'finger of God'.

★ **Museu do Índio** (
→ *Rua das Palmeiras, 5 Tel. 2286-8899 Tue-Fri 9am–5.30pm, Sat-Sun* One of Brazil's most beautiful collections o indigenous art, assem by the Funai (Nationa Foundation for the Ind It reveals fascinating p made with feathers, a as a whole gallery dev to the Wajãpi, an Ama people who decorate objects and themselv with vegetable dyes.

D

↑ Map E

MUSEU CASA DE RUI BARBOSA

MUSEU CASA DE RUI BARBOSA

↑ Map C

A
B M FLAMENC

AVENI
OSVALE
CRUZ

RUA JUCANÃ
RUA B. TÁVORA
R. DE ABREU
R. D. DEABRÃ
RUA BAMBINA
R. MUNIZ BARRETO
PRAIA DE BOTAFOGO
DAS NAÇÕES UNIDAS
PRAIA DE BOTAFOGO
AV

MORRO
MUNDO
NOVO

ENSEA
DE BOTAM

1 MIRANTE
DONA MARTA

RUA FERNANDES
RUA MIN.

MUSEU
CASA DE
RUI BARBOSA

RUA SÃO CLEMENTE
RUA HUMAITÁ
R. REAL GRANDEZA
RUA DAS PALMEIRAS
RUA CONDE DE IRAJÁ
R. PINHEIRO GUIMARÃES

MUSEU
DO ÍNDIO ★

RUA V. DA PÁTRIA
RUA DONA MARIANA
RUA HENRIQUE DE NOVAES
RUA MENA BARRETO

R. DUNTEL
BOTAFOGO M

BOTAFOGO

RUA DA PASSAGEM
R. A. QUINTELA

RIO
PLAZA
SHOPPING
AV
R. B. ROXELEN
RUA GEN
SEVERIANO
AV. L. SODRÉ

2

RUA GENERAL POLIDORO
RUA ÁLVARO RAMOS

RIO SUL
SHOPPIN
CENTER

CEMITÉRIO
SÃO JOÃO BATISTA

MORRO DE
SÃO JOÃO

LAD. DO LEME
RUA C. PEIXOTO
R. GEN. C. DE AGUI
RUA G

RUA
EUCLIDES
DA ROCHA

RUA
TEN. MARONES
DE GUSMÃO

LADEIRA
DOS TABAJARAS

RUA SIQUEIRA
RUA F. DE MAGALHÃES
D. VIEIRA
RUA SANTA CLARA
R. M. F. BRAGA

SIQUEIRA
CAMPOS
M
CAMPOS

ARCOVERDE
ARCOVERDE M

RUA RONALD
DE CARVALHO
R. PRADO
COPACABANA

AV. P

3

MORRO
DOS
CABRITOS

RUA TONELERO
RUA BARATA RIBEIRO
AV. N. S. DE COPACABANA
R. LINS

COPACABANA
PALACE

AVENID

POST

R. JUNQUEIRA
RUA JRA
ÍNGRESE
R. P. LOUREIRO
R. B. RIBEIRO
RUA C. RAMOS
DE COPACABANA
JOÃO FERREIRA
ATLÂNTICA
R. BOLÍVAR

★ POSTO 3

COPACABANA

POSTO 4

4

The Sugarloaf Mountain looms majestically over the Guanabara Bay, on a peninsula that is partly occupied by the army but also boasts one of Rio's most enchanting neighborhoods: Urca, built alongside a coastal promenade. The densely populated district of Botafogo extends to the west, its congested streets around the Cobal market offering a host of lively restaurants. To the east lies the mythical Copacabana: a victim of its own success and uncontrolled development, *Princezinha do mar* strives to project a rebellious image – its democratic beach attracts sun-worshippers from all social classes, while its clubs track the latest underground trends.

PRAIA VERMELHA

MARIUS CRUSTÁCEOS

RESTAURANTS

Praia Vermelha (D C2)
→ *Praça General Tibúrcio (Círculo Militar da Praia Vermelha)*
Tel. 2543-7284 Daily 11am–2am (midnight Sun)
This terrace near the cable-car station overlooks the sea, with the Sugarloaf Mountain in the background. International cuisine by day and pizzas straight from the log-fired oven after 6pm. Expect to wait for a table at the weekend: not only is the moonlight on the bay a draw in its own right, but also priority is given to members of the military club! Main course R$20.

Sindicato do Chopp (D A4)
→ *Av. Atlântica, 3806*
Tel. 2523-4644
Daily 9am–4am
The popular terrace of the 'beer syndicate' finds its lunchtime customers eating in tangas and swimsuits, their feet still coated in sand! Brazilian food in copious portions (*feijoada* on Saturdays). Main course R$20–35.

Amir (D B3)
→ *Rua Ronald de Carvalho, 55-C. Tel. 2275-5596*
Daily noon–11pm
Over the years, Amir, run by a Lebanese couple, has earned a reputation as the best Middle Eastern restaurant in the city. The menu includes *kebbe*, *kafta*, falafel, shawarma and couscous. Main course R$22.

Yorubá (D B2)
→ *Rua Arnaldo Quintela, 94*
Tel. 2541-9387
Tue-Fri 7pm–midnight, Sat 2–11pm, Sun noon–7pm
In a small blue dining room strewn with *pitangas* leaves, Neide Santos elevates Afro-Brazilian cooking to the realm of art. Do not miss the *Ebubu fulô*: fish in homemade coconut milk with ginger, smoked prawns and mashed plantain. The portions are big enough to share. Set menu R$60.

Don Camillo (D A4)
→ *Av. Atlântica, 3056*
Tel. 2549-9958
Daily noon–midnight
One of the few reliable restaurants on the Copacabana beachfront. Italian specialties, with musical accompaniment (9pm) from a quartet of bass, violin, accordion and singer. Set menu R$50.

Marius Crustáceos (D C3
→ *Av. Atlântica, 290-A*
Tel. 2104-9002
Daily noon–midnight
An exhilarating seafood

E DANÇA CARLINHOS DE JESUS · ESPAÇO UNIBANCO · LE BOY, LA GIRL

rodízio: grilled fish and crustaceans are served at the table, while oysters, sea urchins and shellfish rest on beds of ice. *Rodízio* (buffet) R$97.

DANCE, GYM

Casa de Dança Carlinhos de Jesus (D B2)
→ Rua Álvaro Ramos, 11
Tel. 2541-6186
Take the plunge into samba, *forró* and paired dancing in general at Rio's most famous school. Classes in Portuguese (R$60/hr) and English (R$100/hr).

Bodytech (D A4)
→ Av. Nossa Senhora de Copacabana, 801
Tel. 3816-1791
Mon-Fri 6am–11pm;
Sat 9am–1pm, 5–8pm;
Sun 9am–2pm
This ultramodern sports club has state-of-the-art equipment, designed to create perfect bodies to show off on the beach! Day pass R$80.

BARS, MOVIES

Cobal (D A2)
→ Rua Voluntários da Pátria, 446. Daily 8am–2am
By day, this is a fruit and vegetable market; by night, the ten bars in the vicinity set out their tables on this old parking lot and offer snacks with musical accompaniment. *Choro* concerts Sunday nights.

Pérgula (D B3)
→ Av. Atlântica, 1702
Tel. 2548-7070
Daily 7am–midnight
The supremely chic café-restaurant in the Copacabana Palace offers its turquoise swimming pool as a surrealistic setting for a late drink or an early breakfast.

Cervantes (D B3)
→ Av. Prado Júnior, 335-B
Tel. 2542-9287
Tue-Sun noon–4am
After a night of revelry in the nightclubs of 'Copa', insomniacs pile into Cervantes. The main attraction is the enormous roast pork and pineapple sandwiches, served until closing time.

Espaço Unibanco (D A2)
→ Rua Voluntários da Pátria, 35 Tel. 3221-9221
This cultural center is a haven for lovers of art movies, as well as being a perfect place to kill time when it is raining! Apart from screening acclaimed movies with subtitles, the complex comprises a gourmet café and a store selling records and books (old and new) – ideal for whiling away the time before your movie begins.

Bip Bip (D A4)
→ Rua Almirante Gonçalves, 50-D Tel. 2267-9696
Daily 6.30pm–1am
There are no waiters and no menu here – just an owner who is something of a local legend. On Sundays, musicians and enthusiasts take part in the traditional *roda de samba* until 10pm. When you want a drink, just help yourself from the fridge at the back. *Chorinho* on Tuesdays.

NIGHTCLUBS

Fosfobox (D A3)
→ Rua Siqueira Campos, 143-22 A . Tel. 2548-7498
Fri-Sat 10pm–5am
(11pm Sat)
In the basement of a shopping mall, Fosfobox pulsates to the beats of techno, electro and Brazilian funk. Keep an eye on the program (some Sundays, there are after-hour sessions until 9am).

Le Boy, La Girl (D A5)
→ Rua Raul Pompéia, 102
Tel. 2513-4993
Fri-Sun 11pm–5am
The two catalysts of Rio's gay nightlife (one female and one male) are obligatory ports of call for many visiting international stars.

Casa da Matriz (D A2)
→ Rua Henrique de Novaes, 107 Tel. 2266-1014
Mon, Thu-Sat 11.30pm–5am
A villa with a variety of settings: dance floors, galleries, outlandish clothes stores, lounge bar etc. Thematic nights (rock, drum 'n' bass), including the mythical *Brazooka* (MPB, samba) on Fridays.

SHOPPING

Mundo Verde (D A4)
→ Av. Nossa Senhora de Copacabana, 630
Tel. 2257-3183 Mon-Sat 9am–8pm (Sat 6pm)
The famous Zen-style chain offers a wide range of products: incense, natural oils and creams, algae, teas, snacks – and express shiatsu sessions at R$10 for 15 minutes.

Modern Sound (D A3)
→ Rua Barata Ribeiro, 502-D
Tel. 2548-5005 Mon-Sat 9am–9pm (8pm Sat)
Rio's biggest music store: a catalog with 50,000 titles, thousands of CDs displayed in racks (vast selection of Brazilian music). Piano bar and free concerts in the Allegro Bistrô (Mon-Fri 1pm and 5pm; Sat noon and 4pm).

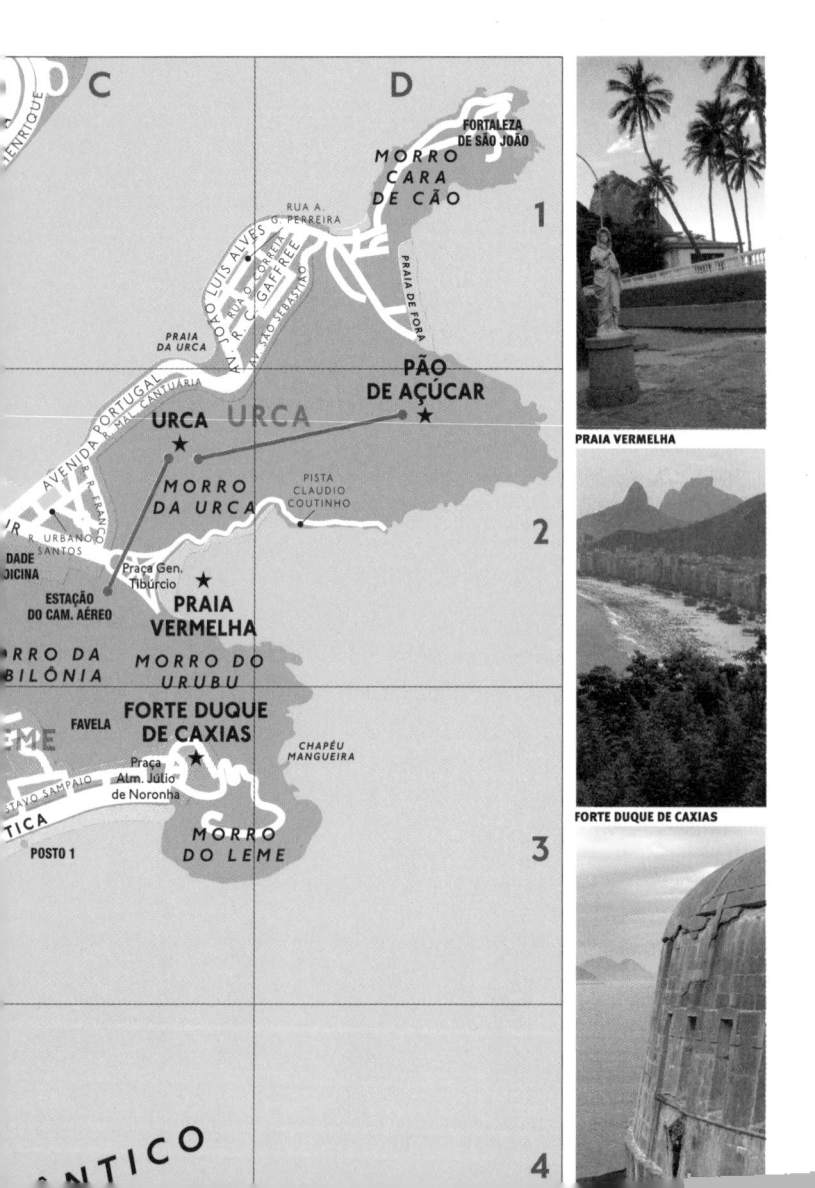

C

D

FORTALEZA
DE SÃO JOÃO

*MORRO
CARA
DE CÃO*

1

RUA A.
G. PERREIRA

PRAIA
DE FORA

*PRAIA
DA URCA*

JOÃO LUIS ALVES
RUA O. CORREIA
R. C. GAFFREE
M. SÃO SEBASTIÃO

**PÃO
DE AÇÚCAR**
★

AVENIDA PORTUGAL
R. MEL. CANTUÁRIA

URCA URCA
★

*MORRO
DA URCA*

PISTA
CLAUDIO
COUTINHO

2

AVENIDA P. R. FRANCO

R. URBANO
SANTOS

IR

DADE
DICINA

Praça Gen.
Tibúrcio

★

**ESTAÇÃO
DO CAM. AÉREO**

**PRAIA
VERMELHA**

RRO DA
BILÔNIA

*MORRO DO
URUBU*

ME

FAVELA

**FORTE DUQUE
DE CAXIAS**
★

CHAPÉU
MANGUEIRA

STAVO SAMPAIO

Praça
**Alm. Júlio
de Noronha**

TICA

POSTO 1

*MORRO
DO LEME*

3

NTICO

4

PRAIA VERMELHA

FORTE DUQUE DE CAXIAS

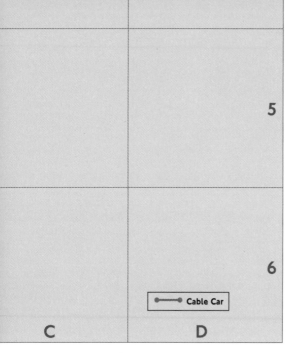

5

6

● Cable Car

C   D

COPACABANA

COPACABANA

rte
opacabana (D A5)
ça Coronel Eugênio
1 Tel. 2521-1032
un 10am–8pm
museum)
ort, built in 1914, now
es the Army Museum.
notice the startling
if you turn your back
e city, you have the
ession that you are
ended over the ocean!
pacabana (D B4)
cabana beach surely
s no introduction.
was once merely an
ched strip of sand
ne elegant around
with the construction
Copacabana Palace,

and became citified in
1950 on completion of
its seafront, the Avenida
Atlântica. In 1969, Burle
Marx designed its
Portuguese-style calçadão
(alternating black and white
paving stones), in the form
of a wave along the edge of
the beach and with
geometrical motifs closer
to the buildings. Here and
there, a few Art-Deco
houses have survived this
series of metamorphoses.
★ **Praia Vermelha (D** D2)
→ Praia Vermelha /
Pista Claudio Coutinho
A tiny beach with red sand,
tucked between Sugarloaf
Mountain and the Morro do

Urubu. On the end near
the mountain, the Pista
Claudio Coutinho, a superb
3-mile promenade, hugs
the rocks overlooking the
sea. It passes through lush
vegetation, where it is not
unusual to spot micos,
the small monkeys that
flourish in Rio's woodland.
Halfway along this walk, a
path climbs through the
forest up to the peak of
Morro da Urca.
★ **Forte Duque**
de Caxias (D C3)
→ Praça Almirante Júlio de
Noronha. Tel. 2275-3122
Sat-Sun and public holidays
9am–5pm
This fort surveys the

entrance to the bay from
the heights of the Morro do
Leme (918 feet). Its strategic
location has endowed it
with magnificent views of
the Sugarloaf Mountain and
the bluish peaks of the Serra
do Mar. Four howitzers still
stand guard, while a café is
on hand to refresh visitors
who complete the bracing
walk to the site. On the
Atlantic side, the half moon
of Copacabana stretches
into the distance and the
outline of the Pedra Dois
Irmãos can also be seen.
At the foot of the fort, Leme
beach offers gentle seas
that attract families from
the neighborhoods.

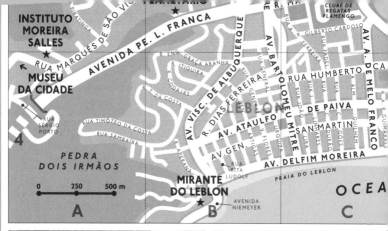

INSTITUTO MOREIRA SALLES

MUSEU DA CIDADE

★ Pedra
do Arpoador (E F4)
This rock plunges into the sea like a small cape. The locals come here to fish or enjoy the views: on one side, the beaches of Ipanema and Leblon; on the other, those of Copacabana and Diabo. The Arpoador beach is a dream for surfers.

★ Ipanema (E E4)
Rio's most fashionable beach was first developed in 1894 and, in 1960, went on to become the epicenter of the bossa nova movement launched by João Gilberto, Vinicuis de Moraes and Tom Jobim: *The Girl from Ipanema* proved to be a worldwide hit (a café of the same name stands on the corner of ruas Vinícius de Moraes and Prudente de Morais). Spectacular sunsets, best appreciated from the heights of Posto 9. The canal connecting the lagoon with the sea marks the separation between Ipanema and Leblon.

★ Mirante
do Leblon (E B4)
A belvedere with a kiosk, graced with splendid views of the beaches of Ipanema and Leblon – especially in the early evening, when the rays of the setting sun glint on the seafront buildings. All this can be enjoyed while sipping a coconut drink on the large wooden terrace lapped by the waves. On the other side, the Sheraton Hotel borders on the *favela* of Vidigal, nestling on the slopes of the Dois Irmãos.

★ Planetário (E B3)
→ *Rua Vice-Governador Rubens Berardo, 100*
Tel. 2274-0096
Museu do Universo:
Tue-Fri 10am–7.30pm (6pm Fri), Sat-Sun 3–7pm
A playful, interactive approach to the solar system, primarily aimed at children: multimedia displays, simulations of space flight etc., as well as a 'Telescope Square' with which to observe the

★ Museu H. Stern (
→ *Rua Garcia d'Ávila, 1*
Tel. 2259-7442
Mon-Fri 10am–6pm
Brazil is the world's fc supplier of precious s and this boasts an unrivalled collection tourmalines (stones t take on a range of col red, blue, yellow, blac – or none at all!).

★ Instituto
Moreira Salles (E A
→ *Rua Marquês de Sã Vicente, 476. Tel. 3284-*
Tue-Sun 1–8pm
Formerly the residenc the landscape painte Redig de Campos, thi

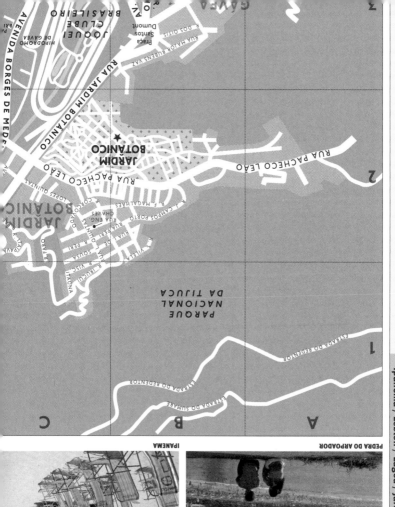

PEDRA DO ARPOADOR

IPANEMA

Ipanema, which merges into Lebon to form a long strip of sand that runs to the foot of the Dois Irmãos, is the beach of gilded youth, pretty girls and a laidback lifestyle. All day long, cyclists and joggers stream along its *calçadão*. After the beach come upmarket shopping facilities, bars spilling onto the sidewalks and café-bookstores open until late at night. Behind the buildings, a heart-shaped expanse of water, the Lagoa Rodrigo de Freitas, is bordered by kiosks offering dinner under the stars. The Jardim Botânico takes advantage of the proximity of the forest to blend into this mass of green stretching to the horizon.

GULA GULA

ZUKA

RESTAURANTS

Paz e Amor (E D4)
→ *Rua Garcia d'Ávila, 173-l, J Tel. 2523-0496 Daily 6am–midnight*
In Rio's most expensive street, the *prato feito* here stands out for its almost ridiculously low prices: fried egg, meat, rice and black beans for only R\$5.50, served all day. À la carte R\$25 (for two).

New Natural (E E4)
→ *Rua Barão da Torre, 173 Tel. 2287-0301 Daily 7am–11pm*
The best value for money in Ipanema. The organic buffet offers purées, (manioc, pumpkin), brown rice, vegetable fritters, sushi, chicken and grilled fish. Buffet R\$12–15.

Gula Gula (E D4)
→ *Rua Aníbal de Mendonça, 132. Tel. 2259-3084 Daily noon–midnight (1am Fri-Sat)*
Pleasant surroundings, reasonable prices and fast service explain why Gula Gula does a roaring trade. Wide range of salads, savory pies and grilled dishes with butter sauce. Set menu R\$20.

Carretão Ipanema (E E4)
→ *Rua Visconde de Pirajá, 112 Tel. 2267-3965 Daily 11am–2am*
The tasty *rodízio* (buffet) of barbecued meat, at a price far more accessible

than that of its nearest competitors, has assured the popularity of this restaurant. *Rodízio* R\$29.

Casa da Feijoada (E E4)
→ *Rua Prudente de Morais, 10. Tel. 2523-4994 Daily noon–midnight*
Feijoada is treated here with exquisite finesse and complemented by 11 varieties of meat, fried manioc flour, Portuguese green cabbage and orange – and a free lime *batida* on the side. *Rodízio* R\$43.

Sushi Leblon (E B4)
→ *Rua Dias Ferreira, 256 Tel. 2274-1342 Mon-Sat 1–4pm 7pm–1am; Sun 1pm–midnight*
This Japanese restaurant with minimalist decor and well-heeled customers is an old favorite of Cariocas. It specializes in sushi, prepared in the middle of the room by a small army of highly dexterous experts. Set menu R\$60. Close by in Rua Dias Ferreira is the excellent Manekineko, the latest addition to Rio's hugely popular sushi scene.

Satyricon (E D4)
→ *Rua Barão da Torre, 192 Tel. 2521-0627 Daily 11.30am–2pm, 7pm–midnight*
Seafood of impeccable freshness dominates a repertoire with distinctive Mediterranean touches. The *gran piatto di mare*

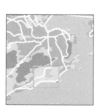

DE FERRO

FEIRA HIPPIE

GILSON MARTINS

(fish carpaccio and shellfish) is exceptional. Main course R$60–80.

Gero (**E** D4)
→ Rua A. de Mendonça, 157 Tel. 2239-8158
Beautiful interior with high ceilings, wooden floors and exposed brick walls. High-class Italian cuisine and all of Rio's VIPS.

Zuka (**E** B4)
→ Rua Dias Ferreira, 233 Tel. 3205-7154 Tue-Fri 1–4pm, 7pm–1am; Sat-Sun 1pm–1am (10pm Sat)
A delight for the eyes as well as the taste buds: fusion cooking with sweet and sour mixtures in a sophisticated setting. Almoço executivo R$29; set menu R$107–127.

BARS

Bar D'Hotel (**E** C4)
→ Marina All Suites Hotel, Ave. Delfim Moreira, 696 Tel. 2172-1100
As hotel bars go, this is a top address for a pre- or post-dinner drink, with fabulous views of Ipanema beach and a no-less fabulous list of cocktails.

Bracarense (**E** C4)
→ Rua José Linhares, 85 Tel. 2294-3549 Daily 7am–midnight (Sun 9am–9pm)
An obligatory port of call after a day on the beach:

chairs on the sidewalk, refreshing beer and prawn empadas.

Arab (**E** C2)
→ Parque dos Patins, Quiosque 7. Tel. 2540-0747 Daily 9am–2.30am
This Syrian-Lebanese stall on the banks of the lagoon is extremely popular for its family atmosphere by day and concerts at night.

Palaphita Kitch (**E** E3)
→ Parque do Cantagalo, Quiosque 20. Tel. 2227-0837 Daily 6pm–2am (3am Fri-Sat)
A small bar-eatery – one of the trendiest in Lagoa.

Hipódromo (**E** B3)
→ Praça Santos Dumont, 108 Tel. 2274-9720 Daily 10am–1am (3am Fri-Sat) www.hipodromo.com.br
Hipódromo has certainly contributed to the popularity of the Baixo Gávea. The end of the square is lined with bars that attract the area's young bohemian set. Arrive early if you want a chance to compete for a table.

Jobí (**E** B4)
→ Av. Ataulfo de Paiva, 1166 Tel. 2274-0547 Daily 9am–4.30am (5.30am Thu-Sat)
Open almost round the clock and always full, Jobí is an institution in Leblon; ideal for a drink, a meal or a caldinho de feijão.

NIGHTCLUBS

Melt (**E** B4)
→ Rua Rita Ludolf, 47 Tel. 2249-9309 Daily 8pm–6am
A very fashionable club with concerts in the early part of the night, and DJs taking over at 11pm.

Dama de Ferro (**E** E3)
→ Rua Vinícius de Moraes, 288. Tel. 2247-2330 Wed-Sun 11pm–5am
This nightclub may look like a bunker, but it has lines outside until the early hours. House music spun by an array of top DJs.

OO (**E** A3)
→ Av. Padre Leonel Franca, 240. Tel. 2540-8041 Tue-Sun 8pm–5am (2am Tue-Wed)
Halfway between a nightclub and a restaurant, the 'Zero Zero' combines contemporary cuisine, refined decor and stylish staff. House music and DJ set after 10pm.

SHOPPING, GYM

Feira Hippie (**E** E4)
→ Praça General Osório Sun 9am–9pm
Local craftspeople meet here every week to sell colorful terracotta dolls, jewelry etc.

Armazém do Café (**E** B4)
→ Rua Rita Ludolf, 87-B

Tel. 2259-0170 Daily 8am–midnight (Fri-Sat 1am)
Enticingly aromatic coffees from Mina Gerais, ground and packaged on the spot. A good place for breakfast.

Garapa Doida (**E** C4)
→ Rua Carlos Góes, 234-F Tel. 2274-8186 Mon-Sat 11am–8pm (6pm Sat)
This store specializes in cachaça made by traditional methods. Bottles R$15–450.

Toca do Vinícius (**E** E4)
→ Rua Vinícius de Moraes, 129-C. Tel. 2247-5227 Daily 9am–10pm (11pm Dec-March)
Rio's musical heritage (samba, choro, bossa nova, MPB) is celebrated in this record store-museum.

Gilson Martins (**E** D4)
→ Rua Visconde de Pirajá, 462-B. Tel. 2227-6178 Mon-Sat 10am–8pm
Accessories manufactured in Brazil's typical vivid colors – trademark of this up-and-coming designer.

Estação do Corpo (**E** C2)
→ Av. Borges de Medeiros, 1426. Tel. 2219-3135 Mon-Fri 6am–11pm, Sat 9am–9pm, Sun 10am–7pm
Make the most of a rainy day in this very select gym with grass paths and English-speaking staff. Aerobics, yoga, weight training, beauty parlor... Day pass R$50.

PARQUE
DA CATACUMBA ★

AV. E. PESSOA

RUA ARATA RIBEIRO

P. LOUREIRO

RUA BRÃO DE

P. J. DE JULHO

LAGOA
RODRIGO
DE
FREITAS

MORRO DOS
CABRITOS

AV. EPITACIO PESSOA

FAVELA
MORRO DOS
CABRITOS

RUA SANTA CLARA

RUA D. VILLARES

F. D. BRAGA

RUA M.ª DE FIGUEIREDO MAGALHÃES

RUA DA ROCHA

RUA I. DA ROCHA

N. REGIA

D'ARCOSTA

RUA M.ª COSTA

MORRO DA
SAUDADE

R. FONTE DA SAUDADE

BORGES DE MEDEIROS

VILA MACHADO

AV. ALEXANDRE FERREIRA

RUA JARDIM BOTANICO

RUA SERRÃO

FAVELA
MANGUEIRA

RUA VISCONDE E SILVA

R. P. GUIMARÃES

RUA HUMAITA

PARQUE LAGE ★

RUA ALFREDO DUARTE

RUA J. TIBIRIÇA

R. DA GRANDEZA

R. REAL

R. VOLUNTARIOS DA PATRIA

R. EUGENIA

R.VIUVA LACERDA

R.JOÃO AFONSO

R. M. MORGAN

MUSEU
DO INDIO

R. HUMAITA

R. C. ABIRU

R. F. ZIRITT MATTOS BARRETO

CRISTO
REDENTOR

PLANETÁRIO

MIRANTE DO LEBLON

U H. STERN

M BOTÂNICO

PARQUE LAGE

PARQUE DA CATACUMBA

ing with pure, horizon-
es (1951) opens onto a
t patio surrounded by
ns designed by Burle
. It is now a prestigious
al center, with
graphic archives from
9th and 20th centuries.
ctive café.

useu da Cidade (E A4)
→ *rada Santa Marinha, 505
e da Cidade. Tel. 2512-
Park: daily 7am–6pm
um: Tue-Sun 11am–6pm*
ush park, once a coffee
ation, is lined with
aths leading up to the
and the Mata Atlântica
t. On top, the City's
rical Museum is set in
egant 19th-century

villa, with period furniture,
paintings and other
mementos. Do not miss the
controversial chapel of St
John the Baptist, decorated
by the Bahian Carlos Bastos
(c.1970) with saints made to
resemble celebrities such as
Pelé and Caetano Veloso!

★ **Jardim Botânico** (E B2)
→ *Rua Jardim Botânico, 1008
Tel. 2294-9349.
Daily 8am–5pm*
No less than 6,200 tropical
species are preserved in
Rio's Botanical Gardens.
Particularly impressive are
the avenues of palm trees
on the approach to the
gardens, and the
glasshouse with countless

varieties of pineapple
plants. Another striking
feature is the central lake
with its *Victoria regia*, water
lilies growing up to 4 feet in
diameter! The gardens
extend into the Mata
Atlântica, home to the
redwood brazil trees that
give the country its name.

★ **Parque
da Catacumba** (E E2)
→ *Av. Epitácio Pessoa, 3000
Tel. 2521-5540 Daily 8am–5pm*
This park is dotted with open-
air sculptures, some by
Frans Krajcberg, who works
with charred wood from
Amazonia. The stunning
views of the hills and the
lagoon should not obscure

the fact that the park's
creation was only made
possible by the demolition
of a *favela*, whose
inhabitants were transferred
to *Cidade de Deus*. These
days, the City Hall prefers
to integrate the *favelas*
into the urban fabric and
acknowledge them as
neighborhoods.

★ **Parque Lage** (E D2)
→ *Rua Jardim Botânico, 414
Daily 9am–5.30pm*
The last remaining reserve
of the primary forest of
Tijuca, now classified as a
natural park spread over
130 acres. It also contains
the School of Visual Arts
(interesting exhibitions).

OCEANO ATLÂNTICO

4

0   0,5   1 km

A   B   C

CANAL DO P

CANAL DO BACALHAU

RESTINGA DE

ILHA DO FRADE

ESTRAD

CAN DE S

BARR GUAR

ILHA RASA DE GUARATIBA

PRAIA DA BARRA DA TIJUCA

MUSEU CASA DO PONTAL

★ Casa das Canoas (F E1)
→ *Estrada da Canoa, 2310
(take the São Conrado-Maracaí
bus, line 710). Tel. 3322-3581
Tue-Fri 1–5pm*
Oscar Niemeyer's home
(1951) is a masterpiece of
modern architecture that
manages to be both
intimate and monumental.
Its transparencies and
curves compensate for
the uneven terrain and
seem to blend into the
surrounding vegetation.

★ Vista Chinesa (F F1)
→ *Estrada da Vista Chinesa,
Parque da Tijuca*
This pagoda-like pavilion,
studded with dragons'
heads, recalls the presence
of a camp of Chinese
workers enlisted to dig
the roads running through
the Tijuca National Park.
It overlooks both the
ocean and the Rodrigo de
Freitas Lagoon, with its
backdrop of the park's lush
and seemingly endless
vegetation. This green lung
was created in 1861 by
Pedro II, who ordered trees
to be planted on the hills
that had been razed to
grow coffee.

★ Museu do Açude (F D1)
→ *Estrada do Açude, 764
Tel. 2492-2119
Thu-Sun 11am–5pm*
This luxurious neocolonial
residence in the heart of

the Tijuca National Park,
surrounded by Portuguese-
style gardens, was once
the second home of Carlos
Maya, a renowned patron
of the arts. It now contains
his collection of decorative
art: Portuguese furniture,
English silverwork, French
glass, Chinese porcelain
and tiled panels from the
17th-19th c. Do not miss
the gardens, with their
pavilions, fountains, ponds,
sculptures and neoclassical
tiled globes, or the park,
with its display of works
by major contemporary
Brazilian artists (Oiticica,
Resende, de Freitas,
Ramos etc.).

★ Pedra Bonita (F D
→ *Reached via the Estra
da Canoa, in São Conra*
This rock, used as a
launching pad by han
gliders, enjoys a sens
view of the São Conra
beach and the expans
the Tijuca forest. A foc
leads from the parking
to the peak, nearly 2,3
feet high (1 hour).

**★ Floresta
da Tijuca (F** D1)
→ *Praça Afonso Viseu
(take Estr. das Paineiras
Estr. do Redentor, Alta d
Vista neighborhood)
Tel. 2492-5407
Daily 8am–5pm*
The most domesticate

F

CASA DAS CANOAS

VISTA CHINESA

FLORESTA DA TIJUCA

A B C

1

MORRO
DA PANELA

MORRO
DO QUILOMBO

AVENIDA ENGENHEIRO SOUZA FILHO

MORRO
DA MUZEMA

ITANHANGÁ

ESTRADA DA BARRA DA TIJUCA

2

LAGOA DA TIJUCA

ESTRADA DO ITANHANGÁ

ESTRADA DA BARRA DA TIJUCA

MORRO
DO FOCIN

AVENIDA DAS AMÉRICAS

CITTÁ
AMÉRICA

DOWNTOWN
SHOPPING

ILHA DA
GIGÓIA

RUA
CONDE E

CANAL DE MARAPENDI

BARRA
DA TIJUCA

AV. A - LOMBARDI

Praça Des-
Araújo
Jorge

JO

Praça
Prof. Bernardino

AV. MINISTRO IVAN

AV. ÉRICO
VERÍSSIMO

AVENIDA SERNAMBETIBA

★

PRAIA
DA BARRA
DA TIJUCA

PRAIA DA BARRA DA TIJUCA

AVENIDA DO PEPE

PON
DA JOA

3

The National Park of Tijuca, the world's biggest urban forest, classified by UNESCO as a Biosphere Reserve, sets apart Rio's North, South and West zones. It is best explored by car, with a stopover in a restaurant nestling among the trees. Along the Atlantic, it is bounded by Barra da Tijuca, an extraordinary concrete jungle with luxury, gated communities and gigantic shopping malls. The extremely clean beaches become increasingly unspoilt toward the Recreio dos Bandeirantes, Grumari and Prainha. In Barra de Guaratiba, Rio recovers its past as a fishing village!

POINT DE GRUMARI

TIA PALMIRA

RESTAURANTS

**Restaurante
A Floresta** (F D1)
→ Estr. Barão do Bom Retiro (reached via Estr. da Cascatinha)
Tel. 2492-5358
Daily 11am–6pm
Deep in the heart of the Floresta da Tijuca, this old building with worn floors and cracked tiles welcomes entire families on Sundays, attracted by eating an enormous feijoada among the sounds of humming birds and rustling leaves. Main course R$30 (for two).

Guimas (F E2)
→ Estrada da Gávea, 899 (Fashion Mall)
Tel. 3322-5791
Daily noon–midnight
A further excuse to go shopping in the luxurious São Conrado shopping mall. Guimas opens onto the street by means of its pretty glassed-in terrace. The food is elaborate: duck with orange, cinnamon and caramelized onions, excellent homemade pâté. Main course R$35.50–38.50.

Barra Grill (F C3)
→ Av. Ministro Ivan Lins, 314
Tel. 2493-6060
Daily 11.30am–1am

This stronghold of devoted meat-eaters serves selected pieces of meat – picanha from Argentina, lamb from Uruguay – taken straight from the grill and carved at the table. Garnishes include sushi, various salads and Lebanese specialties. Rodízio R$46.90.

Point de Grumari (F D4)
→ Estr. do Grumari, 710
Tel. 2410-1434
Daily noon–6.30pm
(7.30pm Sat-Sun)
Perched above the Restinga de Marambaia, the slither of sand running round the Sepetiba Bay, this restaurant provides an unbeatable view of a landscape virtually unaltered by human hand. The sunsets are particularly spectacular. The house specialty is seafood caldeirada (casserole). Music every day. Main course R$40–60 (for two).

Bira (F C4)
→ Estr. da Vendinha, 68-A
Tel. 2410-8304 Thu-Sun
noon–6pm (8pm Sat-Sun)
Bira is a fisherman who regales customers with his catch. All the dishes are prepared from scratch (expect to wait) and the results are masterly. Added extras: the antics of the marmosets outside and the

ACA DO PEPÊ   K-o8   TOTEM PRAIA

breathtaking view of Restinga de Marambaia. Main course R$95 (for two).

Tia Palmira (**F** C4)
→ Caminho de Souza, 18
Tel. 2410-0549
Tue-Sun 11.30am–7pm
'Aunt' Palmira has made a name for herself through her culinary skills. Customers come from far and wide to try the specialties on her menu. Pride of place goes to seafood, prepared Bahia style (*moqueca*, *vatapá* etc.). Set menu R$49.

BARS

Bar do Oswaldo (**F** C2)
→ Estrada do Joá, 3896 (Praça Des. Araújo Jorge)
Tel. 2493-1840
Daily noon–2.30am
This may not look much from the outside, but many locals reckon its *batidas* are the best in the entire city – and this reputation has remained intact for 60 years! The distinctive flavors include peanut, strawberry and mandarin orange.

Barraca do Pepê (**F** C3)
→ Av. do Pepê, 1276
Tel. 8889-4707
Daily 9am–10pm
The action on the Praia do Barra revolves around this

kiosk, named after its former owner – a surfer who was the first person to think of selling sandwiches on this beach. Pepê may have moved on but his creation is still one of the area's most popular spots. Volleyball matches, large wooden terrace, music stage in summer (Thu-Sun) and a throng of permanently tanned youngsters!

Bar Devassa (**F** C2)
→ Av. Armando Lombardi, 483-A, B. Tel. 2494-7626
Daily 6pm–4am
A contemporary reinterpretation of Rio's traditional *boteco*: home-brewed beer (both lager and bitter), painstaking decoration and extensive menu (try the sausages flambéed in *cachaça*).

Conversa Fiada (**F** C2)
→ Av. Armando Lombardi, 800-J, K (Condado de Cascás). Tel. 2496-3222
Tue-Sat 7pm–1am
This lively bar is unpretentious, seeking only to serve a good chilled beer and a large selection of snacks (kebabs, *empadas*, sausages, cheese, olives) as fuel for relaxed conversation. Its modest ambitions are

superbly fulfilled.

Academia da Cachaça (**F** C2)
→ Av. Armando Lombardi, 800-L (Condado de Cascás)
Tel. 2492-1159
Daily noon–2am. www. academiadacachaca.com.br
This relaxed and open-air Academy sells no less than 60 brands of Brazil's national drink, made by traditional methods. Try it straight, in infusions or in cocktails (ginger-orange, honey-lemon), or with *escondidinho* (mashed manioc and dried meat).

Barril 8000 (**F** A3)
→ Av. Sernambetiba, 8000
Tel. 2433-1730 Daily 4pm–3.30am (2am Sun)
This *choperia* on the beach has a lively atmosphere, enhanced by music: *pagode* (Mon & Thu), MPB, rock (daily from 8pm).

NIGHTCLUBS

Cantinho da Barra (**F** C2)
→ Rua Conde d'Eu, 89
Tel. 2429-3078 Wed-Sun 10pm–4am (6pm Sun)
An intimate concert hall, with an audience aged mainly 18–25. Forró, reggae, *samba de mesa* and other dance rhythms.

Nuth Lounge (**F** C2)
→ Av. Armando Lombardi, 999. Tel. 3153-8595

Daily 10pm–5am
Local celebrities are only too happy to be seen in this chic, rather select nightclub with elegant wood trim and an inner garden. Electronic samba, hip hop, dance and MPB.

WINDSURFING

K-o8 (**F** C3)
→ Av. do Pepê (opposite no. 900). Tel. 2494-4869
Learn to surf, with or without the aid of a sail, in this surfing/windsurfing club located right on the golden sands of the Barra beach. Windsurfing package (8-hr individual tuition) R$950.

SHOPPING

Totem Praia (**F** B2)
→ Av. das Américas, 500 (Downtown Bloco 8, 105)
Tel. 2493-0143 Mon-Sat 10am–10pm, Sun 3–9pm
Beachwear with Indonesian prints for both sexes: shirts, skirts etc.

Maria de Barro (**F** B2)
→ Av. das Américas, 700 (Cittá América Bloco 8, 102-K). Tel. 2132-8436
Mon-Sat 10am–8pm
Practical crafts goods from all over Brazil: vases, terracotta casserole dishes, embroidered cushions.

↑ Map E

J DO AÇUDE

PEDRA BONITA

↑ Map E

D
E
F
1
2
3
ESTRADA DA CASCATINHA
Praça Afonso Viseu
ALTO DA BOA VISTA
MORRO DO QUEIMADO
ESTRADA DONA CASTORINA
PARQUE DA CIDADE
FLORESTA DA TIJUCA
VISTA CHINESA
MUSEU HISTÓRICO DA CIDADE
ESTRADA DA VISTA CHINESA
EST. STA MARINHA
EST. DA GÁVEA
DAS FURNAS
CASA DAS CANOAS
MORRO DO COCHRANE
ESTRADA DA PEDRA BONITA
GÁVEA
ESTRADA DA GÁVEA
AV. F-DE-LIMA
ESTRADA DAS CANOAS
FAVELA DA ROCINHA
PEDRA BONITA
ROCINHA
EST. DAS CANOAS
PEDRA DOIS IRMÃOS
SÃO CONRADO
GÁVEA GOLF
SÃO CONRADO FASHION MALL
VIDIGAL
FAVELA DO VIDIGAL
ESTRADA DA LAGOA-BARRA
AV. PREFEITO MENDES DE MORAIS
AVENIDA NIEMEYER
PEDRA DA GÁVEA
PRAIA DE SÃO CONRADO
ESTRADA DA JOÁ
ELEVADO DAS BANDEIRAS
PRAIA DOS AMORES
PONTA DO MARISCO

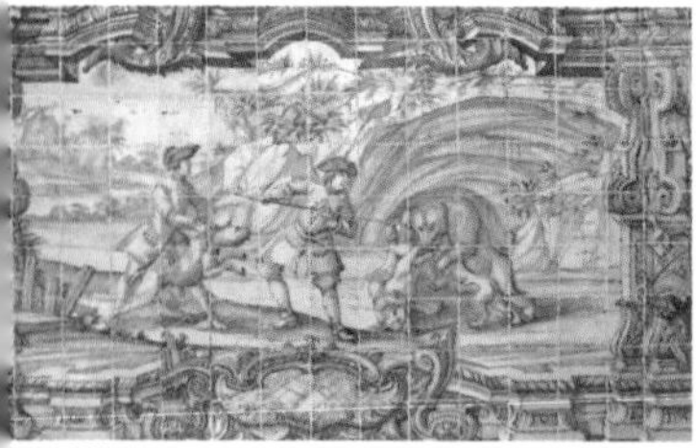

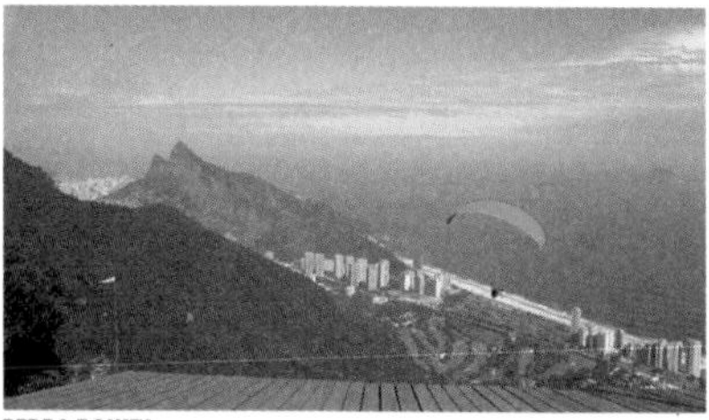

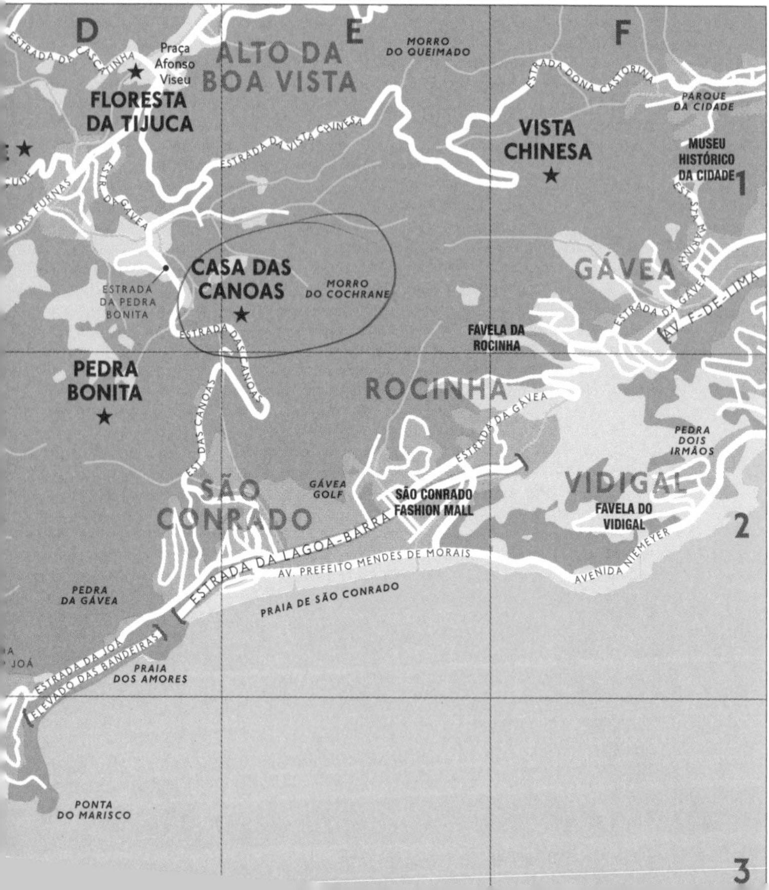

SÍTIO ROBERTO BURLE MARX

MUSEU CASA DO PONTAL

PRAINHA E GRUMARI

PRAIA DO GRUMARI

ILHA DAS PEÇAS

RECREIO DOS BANDEIRANTES

AVENIDA DAS AMÉRICAS

AV. DAS AMÉRICAS

PRAIA DO MACUMBA

PRAINHA

CANAL DO CORTADO

AVENIDA ESTADO DA GUANABARA

D E F

4

PONTAL TIM MAIA

0 1 2 km

...HA

GRUMARI

SÍTIO ROBERTO BURLE MARX

of the Tijuca National ...s distinguished by ...ascatinha de Taunay, ...antic waterfall popular 19th-century artists; ...apela Mayrink, with ...s painted by Cândido ...ari; the Pico da Tijuca ...o feet) and the Pico de ...gaio (3,245 feet).

...aia da Barra
...juca (F B3)
...s line 225 (Praça XV /

...ongest beach in Rio: ...es! To its rear stands ...arra da Tijuca, an ...ishing new town that ...xpanded according to ...verall plans drawn up ...cio Costa. There are

plans afoot to complement it with a City of Music designed by Christian de Portzamparc. One end of the beach forms a nature reserve unspoilt by urban development.

★ **Museu Casa**
do Pontal (F E4)
→ Estrada do Pontal, 3295 (Recreio). From South Rio, bus no. 175/179 to Barrashopping, then bus no. 703 (Barra-Recreio line). Tel. 2490-3278
Tue-Sun 9am-5.30pm
Brazil's finest collection of popular art, enriched over the years by the passionately enthusiastic Jacques Van de Beuque. Highlights include the

terracotta 'monsters' made by Manuel Galdino (1929–96), the naive clay statuettes with human or animal forms, and a collection of erotic figurines.

★ **Sítio Roberto**
Burle Marx (F D3)
→ Estrada da Barra de Guaratiba, 2019.
Frescão bus, Santa Cruz (Via Barra) or Campo Grande (Via Barra) lines
Tel. 2410-1412
Tours by appointment:
Tue-Sat 9.30am and 1.30pm;
Sun 9.30am
The great landscape gardener lived here from 1973 until his death in 1994. A visit to his house

and painting studio reveals his collection of popular art and, above all, the extraordinary glasshouses with over 3,500 species of plants. There is also a lovely 17th-century chapel. One of Rio's hidden treasures.

★ **Prainha**
and Grumari (F E4)
→ Reached by Surf Bus
Daily 7am, 10am, 1pm, 4pm
Tel. 2539-7555
Prainha ('little beach') and the neighboring Grumari are areas protected from construction and off the beaten track, but visitors are rewarded by pristine stretches of white sand.

Transportation in Rio de Janeiro

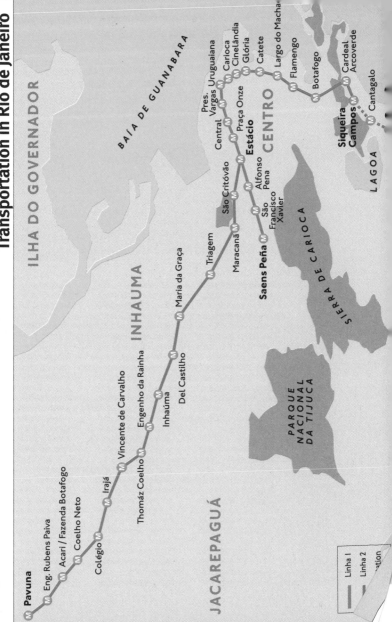

ILHA DO GOVERNADOR

BAÍA DE GUANABARA

INHAÚMA

JACAREPAGUÁ

PARQUE NACIONAL DA TIJUCA

SIERRA DE CARIOCA

CENTRO

LAGOA

Pavuna
Eng. Rubens Paiva
Acari / Fazenda Botafogo
Coelho Neto
Colégio
Irajá
Vicente de Carvalho
Thomáz Coelho
Engenho da Rainha
Inhaúma
Del Castilho
Maria da Graça
Triagem
Maracanã
São Critóvão
São Francisco Xavier
Saens Peña
Afonso Pena
Estácio
Central
Pres. Vargas
Praça Onze
Uruguaiana
Carioca
Cinelândia
Glória
Catete
Largo do Macha
Flamengo
Botafogo
Cardeal Arcoverde
Siqueira Campos
Cantagalo

Linha I
Linha 2
...ation

The letters (**A, B, C**...) correspond to the classification of the different districts.
On their own, the letters refer to an address (restaurant, café, bar, store); when
followed by a star (**A ★**), they refer to a monument or a place to visit.

1º de Março (rua) **A** D2-D3
15 de Novembro (praça)
  A E3
7 de Setembro (rua)
  A C3-D3
Aarão Reis (rua) **B** B3
Açude (estrada do) **F** C1-D1
Adalberto Ferreira (rua)
  E C3-C
Afonso Viseu (praça) **F** D1
Afrânio de Melo Franco
  (avenida) **E** C3-C4
Alberto Campos (rua)
  E E4
Alexandre Ferreira
  (avenida) **E** D2-E2
Alexandre Mackenzie
  (rua) **A** B2-B3
Alfândega (rua da)
  A C3-D3
Alfredo Agache (avenida)
  A E3
Alice (rua) **C** C2-D2
Alm. Alexandrino (rua)
  B A4-C2, **A** A3-C1
Alm. Barroso (avenida)
  A D4-E4, **B** E1
Alm. de Tamandaré (rua)
  C F1
Alm. Gonçalves (rua)
  D A4, **E** F3
Alm. Júlio de Noronha
  (praça) **D** C3
Álvaro Alvim (rua)
  A D4, **B** E1
Álvaro Ramos (rua) **D** B2
Américas (avenida das)
  F A2-B2, E3-F4
Angrense (travessa) **D** A4
Aníbal de Mendonça (rua)
  E C4-D4
Anita Garibaldi (rua) **D** A3
Aprazível (rua) **B** B4-C4
Araújo Porto Alegre (rua)
  A D4-E4, **B** E1
Arcos (rua dos) **B** D1-D2
Armando Lombardi
  (avenida) **F** B2-C2

Arnaldo Quintela (rua)
  C E4, **D** B2
Assembléia (rua da)
  A D3-E3
Ataúlfo de Paiva
  (avenida) **E** B4-C4
Atlântica (avenida)
  D A4-C3, **E** F3-F4
Augusto Severo
  (avenida) **B** E2-E3
Áurea (rua) **B** B3
Bambina (rua) **C** D3, **D** A1
Bandeiras (elevado das)
  F D2-D3
Barão da Torre (rua)
  E D4-E4
Barão de Ipanema (rua)
  E F3
Barão de Jaguaripe (rua)
  E D4-E4
Barão do Flamengo (rua)
  C E1
Barata Ribeiro (rua)
  D A4-B3, **E** F3
Barra da Tijuca
  (estrada da) **F** C2
Barra de Guaratiba
  (estrada da) **F** D3-D4
Bartolomeu de Gusmão
  (avenida) **A** A1
Bartolomeu Mitre
  (avenida) **E** B3-C4
Beira Mar (avenida) **B** E2
Bento Lisboa (rua)
  B D4, **C** E1
Bolívar (rua) **D** A4, **E** F3
Borges de Medeiros
  (avenida) **E** C3- D2
Botafogo (praia de)
  C E3, **D** B1
Bragança (beco de) **A** D2
Buenos Aires (rua)
  A B3-D3
Cândido Mendes (rua)
  B C3-D3
Canoas (estrada das)
  F D2-E2
Cardeal D. Sebastião

Leme (rua) **B** B2-B3
Carioca (largo da) **A** D4
Carioca (rua da) **A** C4-D3
Carlos Brandt (rua) **B** C3
Carlos Góes (rua) **E** C4
Cascatinha (estrada da)
  F D1
Catete (rua do) **B** F3-F4,
  C E1
Churchill (avenida)
  A E4-F4, **B** F1
Claudio Coutinho (pista)
  D D2
Comércio (travessa do)
  A E2
Conceição (rua da) **A** C3
Conde D'eu (rua) **F** C2
Conde de Baependi (rua)
  C D2-E2
Conde de Irajá (rua) **D** A2
Constante Ramos (rua)
  D A4
Constituição (rua da)
  A C3-C4
Coronel Eugênio Franco
  (praça) **D** A5
Correia Dutra (rua)
  B D4-E4
Cosme Velho (rua) **C** C2-C3
Cruz Vermelha (praça)
  A B4, **B** B1
Cupertino Durão (rua)
  E C4
Debret (rua) **A** D4-E4, **B** E1
Delfim Moreira (avenida)
  E B4-C4
Dércio Vilares (rua)
  D A3, **E** F2
Desembargador Aráujo
  Jorge (praça) **F** C2-C3
Dias Ferreira (rua) **E** B4
Djalma Ulrich (rua) **D** A4
Dom Gerardo (rua) **A** D2
Domingos Ferreira (rua)
  D A4
Dr. Julio Otoni (rua) **C** C2
Eng. Freyssinet (avenida)
  C A1-A2

Eng. Graça Aranha (rua)
  E B3-B4
Eng. Souza Filho
  (avenida) **F** A1-B1
Epitácio Pessoa
  (avenida) **E** E2-E3
Erasmo Braga (avenida)
  A E3
Érico Veríssimo (avenida)
  F C3
Estado da Guanabara
  (avenida) **F** D4-E4
Evaristo da Veiga (rua)
  A D4, **B** D1
Farme de Amoedo (rua)
  E E4
Faro (rua) **E** C2
Figueiredo de Magalhães
  (rua) **D** A3-A4, **E** F2
Flamengo (praia do)
  B E4, **C** F1-F2
Floriano Peixoto (praça)
  A D4, **B** E1
Francisco Bicalho
  (avenida) **A** B1
Francisco Negrão de
  Lima (avenida) **F** F1
Francisco Otaviano (rua)
  D A5, **E** F4
Francisco Pinto (praça)
  A C4, **B** D1
Francisco Sá (rua)
  D A5, **E** F4
Frassinetti (rua) **C** A1
Frei Caneca (rua)
  A A4-B4, **B** B1
Furnas (estrada das) **F** D1
Garcia d'Àvila (rua) **E** D4
Gávea (estrada da)
  F D1-F1
Gen. Artigas (rua) **E** B4
Gen. Caldwell (rua)
  A A3-A4, **B** B1
Gen. Glicério (rua) **C** C2-C3
Gen. Justo (avenida)
  A F4, **B** F1
Gen. Osório (praça)
  E E4-F4

COMBIS

SEALINKS FROM PRAÇA XV

Ipanema Plaza (**E** E4)
→ *Rua Farme de Amoedo, 34*
Tel. 3687-2000
www.ipanemaplazahotel.com
Superb location, attentive service, impeccable rooms. Spectacular view of the sea from the pool on the top floor. R$389.

Sheraton (**F** F2)
→ *Av. Niemeyer, 121*
Tel. 2529-1144
www.sheraton-rio.com
The idyllic location in a creek makes this Rio's only hotel with its feet literally in the sand. If staying here is not feasible, you can drop in for a drink by the pool, set on a virtually private beach. All the rooms enjoy sea views. R$400.

Hotel Marina Palace (**E** C4)
→ *Av. Delfim Moreira, 630*
Tel. 2172-1000 / 1001
www.hotelmarina.com.br
Extremely luxurious four-story hotel by the same

owners as the Marina All Suites. It overlooks Leblon beach and the best situated rooms have the sea on the horizon, as well as plenty of space. Panoramic restaurant. R$412 (without breakfast).

LUXURY HOTELS

La Maison (**E** A4)
→ *Rua Sérgio Porto, 58*
Tel. 3205-3585
www.chicretreats.com
This large, elegant white villa opens onto an unforgettable panorama of the lagoon, beaches and statue of Christ. Five luxury suites, all with a private terrace. A hideaway popular with stars keen to stay out of the limelight. Exquisite but unfussy service. €200 / R$590.

Marina All Suites (**E** C4)
→ *Av. Delfim Moreira, 696*
Tel. 2172-1100 / 1001
www.hotelmarina.com.br

The latest arrival, with suites created by top designers. Do not miss the extremely chic Bar d'Hotel, with its stunning view of the coastline. R$700 without breakfast.

Ceasar Park (**E** D4)
→ *Av. Vieira Souto, 460*
Tel. 2525-2500
www.caesarpark-rio.com
The most famous of the big hotels, in a highly fashionable part of Ipanema. R$829 without breakfast.

Copacabana Palace (**D** B3)
→ *Av. Atlântica, 1702*
Tel. 2548-7070
www.copacabanapalace.com
The luxurious hotel that first brought pleasure-seekers to Copacabana has lost none of its glamour. Heads of state, movie stars and anyone famous (and rich) have been staying at the 'Copa' for 70 years. R$1,100.

SEALINKS

Estação das Barcas (**A** E3)
→ *Praça XV de Novembro*
Several ferry and catamaran services to Niterói and Paquetá.
'Barcas' (ferry)
→ *Tel. 2533-7524*
Niterói: daily, hourly from midnight to 6am; R$1.85
Paquetá: daily 5.15am–11pm (ten departures/day); R$2.90 (R$4 Sat-Sun)
Catamarã (Catamaran)
→ *Tel. 2533-2211*
Niterói: Mon-Fri 7.10am–8.45pm; every 20 mins; R$4. Paquetá: Mon-Fri 10am–4pm (9am Sat-Sun); every 2 hours

TAXIS

Yellow cabs
→ *Starting fare R$3.30*
Very plentiful; the most practical way of getting around.
Radio Taxi
→ *Starting fare R$4.20*
Coopertramo
→ *Tel. 2560-2022*
Coopatur
→ *Tel. 2573-1009*

CAR

Fast driving and almost total absence of road signs: prudence is required! At night, drivers go through red lights (slowly!). It is customary to give R$1 or 2 to the person who watches over your parked car.
Rental
→ *In the airports;*
on Av. Princesa Isabel (Copacabana)
Around R$150/day.

TRAM ('BONDE')

Tram station (B D1)
→ *Estação de bondes,
Rua Lélio Gama, Carioca
subway station*
Tel. 2240-5709 Daily
6am–11pm; every 15 mins
Two lines from Largo da
Carioca to Santa Teresa:
toward Largo das Neves
(Paula Mattos) or
Corcovado (Silvestre).

COMBIS

The combis (shared
station wagons) work as
cooperatives to make up
for transport shortfalls in
some areas (particularly
in the West and North
zones).

www.windsorhoteis.com
A recent addition to the
Windsor chain, this
smoked-glass box
proposes far more
accessible prices than its
stablemates on Avenida
Atlântica. Excellent
location, in a block
comprising beach houses,
ten minutes from Ipanema
on foot. Modern comfort
geared toward business
travelers. R$200.
**GranDarrell Ouro
Verde Hotel (D** B3)
→ *Av. Atlântica, 1456*
Tel. 2543-4123
www.dayrell.com.br
This Art-Deco hotel, built
right on the Copacabana
beach, has known days of
greater glory but, despite
being rundown (worn
carpets), it has preserved
many of the virtues of
grand old hotels: spacious
rooms (124 square feet),
chandeliers and silver
cutlery! And, for an extra

R$60, you can enjoy
a view of the sea. R$210.
Hotel Novo Mundo (C F1)
→ *Praia do Flamengo, 20*
Tel. 2105-7000
*www.hotelnovomundo-
rio.com.br*
The Novo Mundo looks
unexciting from outside but
its conference rooms and
proximity to the city center
– next to the gardens of the
Palácio da República,
opposite the Aterro – make
it popular with business
travelers. The prettiest
rooms overlook the
Sugarloaf Mountain; the
cheaper ones are showing
signs of wear. R$223.

R$240 TO R$300

Ipanema Inn (E D4)
→ *Rua Maria Quitéria, 27*
Tel. 2523-6092
This small hotel on a
human scale (56 rooms)
benefits from a central
location, near Ipanema's

top restaurants and stores.
Simple but well-equipped
rooms. R$242.
Hotel Flórida (C F1)
→ *Rua Ferreira Viana, 69*
Tel. 2195-6800
www.windsorhoteis.com
A good place to stay in
Flamengo, popular with
with business travelers for
its conference center but
also because it offers free
local calls, free Internet
access and free parking.
The rooms are a bit lifeless
but extremely comfortable
and well maintained. The
swimming pool on the top
floor enjoys view of both
the Sugarloaf Mountain
and the Corcovado. R$263
(incl. taxes).
Portinari Hotel (D A5)
→ *Rua Francisco Sá, 17*
Tel. 3222-8800
www.hotelportinari.com.br
Each of the 11 floors of this
elegant hotel has been
decorated by a different
Brazilian designer – so you

can choose warm or cold
colors, minimalism or
exuberance. Opposite
Posto 6, not far from
Ipanema. Very friendly
service. R$275.

R$300 and over

Hotel Glória (B E3)
→ *Rua do Russel, 632*
Tel. 2555-7272
www.hotelgloriario.com.br
When it was built in 1922
for the celebrations of the
centenary of Brazilian
independence, this hotel
was one of the most
prestigious in Rio. Its
ornamentation now has
a quaint charm – period
furniture, high ceilings,
tapestries, moldings –
but all this is forsaken
in the cheaper rooms
in the modern annex.
Superb views of the bay
and the Sugarloaf Mountain
from the swimming pool.
R$300.